Cycling Along Europe's Rivers

Bicycle Touring Made Easy and Affordable

Over 25 Interesting, Historic, and Cultural Rides

Rhine, Danube, Elbe, Loire Rivers and More

Companion book to the European Bikeline Map Guides

By: Michael J. Lyon

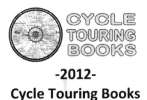

-2012-
Cycle Touring Books

Cover Design by
Eric Anderson and Stephen James Price
Cover Photo: Spay on the Rhine

Published By:
Cycle Touring Books
www.cycletouringbooks.com

To my wife Kusavadee, for understanding why I love these rides, and to my 8 year old son, Joshua – who I am looking forward to spending the next decades riding together in Europe!

To my parents for their loving support all these years.

Finally, I want to thank my Uncle Harvey Lyon, for introducing me to touring and being my riding companion all these years.

Table of Contents

PREFACE

By Harvey Lyon:

At 86, I have been touring in Europe for over 40 years. When I was younger, and there was an iron curtain, I bicycled solo behind it during several summers, wherever they'd let me in with a bike, without good maps or plentiful rivers, pretty much taking it as it came.

But back in 1994 my nephew, Mike, invited me to come on a different type of trip — along Europe's rivers through a more structured, yet still opportunistic way of traveling. Carrying the wonderful Esterbauer guide books, and more recently adding his magic box (Garmin Bike GPS), I came to love this way of touring. The first year he brought the magic box, I asked, smugly, "Mike, if the river's on our left in the morning, and it's still on our left at the end of the day, how wrong could we have gone?" But I grew to appreciate its usefulness in allowing us to adjust our route, and find where we needed to go, down to the meter, from towns, to hotels, to restaurants, to bike stores.

As we refined our approach to river riding over the years, we came to believe that this is really the best way to tour Europe in many ways. Mike's got this approach down to a science now, which allows an older guy to still do a 400 mile bike trip — it's really an approach for everyone. He'll show you how in this book.

The information is solid, practical, and well-organized. But what's really there for you is what's there for us: we've loved doing these trips. So will you.

INTRODUCTION

On a sunny late August afternoon I was rolling through lush vineyards in the heart of Austria's Wachau region when I passed a small stand selling the area's specialized produce. I stopped, deposited my Euro in the can, and devoured a handful of the most favorable grapes I had ever tasted. I stood there enjoying the view, a deep blue sky, the Danube River below to my right, the famous early 18th century Melk Abby behind me, and the outline of the beautiful medieval city of Durnstein around the bend. As far as I could see, the valley was planted with row upon row of grapes destined for the region's famous wines. But these grapes were for me. Charged up, I remounted my bike and pumped with extra energy through this most beautiful of bike trails— a black ribbon winding through the green landscape. That night, relaxing in our hotel where Richard the Lionheart took a rest during the Crusades, my mind's eye replayed that day's enchanting trek, and I smiled.

A highlight of each of the last 18 years has been my 8-14 day self-guided cycling tour along Europe's grand rivers. I am writing this book because many have asked me how to undertake these trips and experience these adventures. They are often surprised just how easy and inexpensive these rides can be with our approach, and how they are suitable for all types of riders. I have tried to put together a book that is practical and easy to follow —a "how to" approach. I hope you can also start enjoying these wonderful adventures to Europe!

The key considerations for planning the types of trips recommended in this book are: (1) keeping the trips to a reasonable period of time so they can be completed during limited vacation periods, (2) making them relatively low cost, not like the standard organized trips that can cost three to six times more, (3) finding interesting and varied locations, (4) identifying easy access points, such as international airports for starting and ending a trip, and good train service along the routes, and (5) selecting routes that are generally flat— which means riding along rivers!

The result has been a series of fantastic adventures exploring some of the most interesting areas in Europe. Our approach and choice of routes makes our rides accessible and appropriate for riders of all levels and age groups, and for participants with limited or more expansive budgets.

These trips are relatively simple to plan and leave riders with the flexibility to explore and improvise. We fly into a European airport (and out of the same or different airports, depending on the route), and often set off right from the terminal without reservations along a route we have chosen. We carry rear panniers (not front panniers) and generally stay in modest (2-3 star) hotels. We do not camp, which goes a long way to keeping our loads manageable. We typically cover 40-50 miles per day and have time to explore many of the great sites, enjoy a leisurely lunch, and of course partake in stops at the many fine pastry shops we find along the way!

In addition to international airfare, we budget about $110 to $140 per day (less if sharing a room), including hotel, food, incidentals, admissions, and local transportation (such as an occasional train or boat ride to skip a bit of territory). We always bring our own bikes.

Our great discovery was that riding along Europe's rivers provides for superb touring. Most of Western Europe's major rivers have well-developed and marked bike trails. European civilization generally developed along these rivers, so river rides provide the opportunity to visit many fascinating cities (both large and small), castles, monasteries, vineyards, museums, and fortresses. Distances between stops are relatively short because these river towns developed when travel was slower and distances were consequently relatively longer.

This book focuses on rides along three main European rivers, various routes that connect these rivers, and a few smaller rivers that connect or intersect with these rivers. These major rivers are the Rhine, the Danube, and the Elbe. Together, these rivers form a virtual circle in the heart of Europe, with Germany at the center, and include sections that also can take riders into Holland, Austria, the Czech Republic, Hungary, France, and Switzerland. I have also provided a few routes that can take you along major French and Italian rivers.

One caveat: **This book does not provide the turn-by-turn routes that some guides do.** I do not think this standard approach is particularly useful for the rides outlined in this book given a variety of factors, including:

- GPS, which has fundamentally changed cycle touring.
- The generally well-marked routes recommended in this book.
- The detailed maps provided in the Bikeline companion guide series.
- The route guidance provided by the rivers themselves.

Rather than detailed directions, this book provides recommended trip routes, general daily miles, proposed overnight stops, special recommendations in certain places, and other route features — all that is necessary for deciding where you would like to ride and how to approach the trip.

I hope you enjoy the book — it can provide you with a virtual lifetime of bike touring options in Europe.

I want to thank the Esterbauer Bikeline guide company for producing its excellent series of guidebooks that have served at the core of many of our trips, and for permitting me to use various maps from these guides in this book.

Finally, and importantly, I want to give special appreciation to my uncle, Harvey Lyon, for introducing me to cycle touring and being my long-time cycling companion. At 86, and still touring with me using this approach, Harvey shows us all that cycle touring can be a lifelong passion.

PART ONE

Overview

Why Ride in Europe

Many Americans never have the pleasure of cycling in Europe. This type of touring is often perceived as complicated and costly, and just not feasible. I hope that after reading this book you will agree that touring in Europe is something you will want to try.

While I also enjoy riding around the U.S., Europe offers special advantages:

- Well-developed and marked bike trails that allow riders to stay away from traffic even when riding from city to city.
- Historic sites such as old churches and castles.
- Relatively short distances between sites and cities.
- Good rail infrastructure along riding routes.
- River tour boats along many routes.
- Lower cost basic, yet clean, accommodations. We often find hotels for half the price of a normal U.S. limited-service hotel chain room.
- Interesting and different cultures.
- Great food. We have great food also in the U.S., of course, but eating local cuisine is one of the pleasures of European touring.

Cycling Along Europe's Rivers

Riding Europe's Rivers: Touring Made Easy

The best part of touring in Europe is the amazing network of bike trails along many of Europe's rivers. Development along Europe's rivers long preceded other forms of transportation, such as rail or highway transportation. Many European rivers are navigable and inter-connected. They continue to play critical roles in transportation, shipping, commerce, and tourism, and have significant infrastructure and interesting sites in many places.

One of the most important advantages of riding along the rivers is that the routes are **generally flat.** This is a critical element for making these rides easy and accessible to riders of various abilities. Climbing hills is challenging when loaded down with the weight of rear panniers. We avoid hills, which does limit our routes to some extent, but this approach allows us to ride further and with a more diverse group. Given the advantages of river touring, I think generally avoiding hills and some venues is a reasonable trade-off.

Here is a summary of some of the reasons we like to tour along rivers:

- Great bike trails that are part of organized and often well-marked routes.
- Most routes are paved and without car traffic, but some sections may be unpaved and others may involve riding on smaller roads.
- Easy navigation, with the river as the ultimate guide.
- Good logistics, given that rail lines often run near rivers, providing easy access to our "sag" support system.
- Many rivers have boats that follow the cycling routes. These boats usually allow bikers aboard, providing a great way to take a break for lunch (while cruising) and skip a section of the ride. These boats often travel through some of the most scenic parts of a river, providing a relaxing way to experience the river's beauty and sites from a different perspective than possible from the bike.

- Many towns, both small and large, along the route. Many of Europe's most interesting cities are along rivers. Rivers also served as trading routes, which helped make many even smaller towns prosperous. This has left an interesting historic and architectural legacy.
- Relatively short distances between towns and sites, given that cities were built when transpiration was slower, and needed to be closer together.
- Rivers can pass through gorges, providing stunning views and castles, monasteries, and vineyards along the side hills.
- Rivers often host wine country, providing a great opportunity to experience many different local European wines along the route, and even chance to tour wineries in various locations.
- Oh yes, did I mention that the trails are generally flat!

Cycling Along Europe's Rivers

The Busy and Interesting Rhine River

Typical Path along River

Preparing For Ride

Who Can Ride and How Far

Touring along Europe's rivers is something that everyone can enjoy. You don't need to be a professional rider! Or even the best rider in your weekend group. We usually figure that riding fully loaded on these flat trails is equivalent to losing one gear on your bike (i.e., you ride at a speed with about the same amount of energy as if you were in one higher gear not loaded.) That means that even casual riders can ride 20 miles per day and take their time along the route, while others can choose to ride 50 or more miles per day.

- **Ages:** All Ages can participate. I have been riding with my uncle all these years, starting when he was 66, and continuing — he is 86 now. At the other end of the spectrum, I am taking my 8 year old this year.
- **Ability**: Novice through Expert. This book outlines a strategy that will support both expert and novice riders, and everyone in between. Rides can be tailored to different levels of riders with various types of interests, riding experience, and intensity.
- **Groups**: Riders of different levels can tour together. Riders that want to ride less can use ferry touring boats or trains to skip sections of a day's ride, and meet other riders down the route or at the final destination.
- **Kids**: These rides are well-suited to riding with kids and families. Off-road trails are the norm, and the roads that are unavoidable are low traffic (and if not, they can be avoided).There are many interesting sites along the routes providing fun and educational stops. Younger kids can ride in trailers behind parents, although I think that there is a limit to how far you can go in a day with this method and keep your kids (and you) from going crazy— maybe 25 miles per day or so.
- **Kids and Couples on Tandems:** Tandems have special distance and speed advantages on these flat routes, avoiding the tough tandem hills! Tandems can also be a good option for both couples and kids. This year I am riding with my 8 year old on a special tandem where he can sit and pedal in a recumbent seat in the front, with

seatbelts, and I steer in the rear. We generally rode about 30-40 miles per day.

- **Non-Riders**: Non-riders can also join the trip. Non-riders can move from one location to another by train on many routes. There are also river boat systems in certain areas that can be used by non-riders. Of course, it's possible to rent a car and follow the route, something that provides maximum flexibility, but that will increase expense. Renting a car or van can be a good option if multiple people are non-riders, and they can share the expense, driving, and navigation.

- **Distances:** Our general distances are 35-55 miles per day. For families and people who want to take their time, a 20 mile per day schedule works along most of the rivers. We generally do not ride more than 55 miles per day, since we find that riding more than this distance does not give us time to explore the sites, stop for a nice coffee and pastry every so often, and have a relaxing lunch. We also don't like to get into a town after 4 PM since we don't usually have hotel reservations, and getting in late can make it harder to find rooms in some towns during busy periods.

How to Prepare

Preparing for your trip is half the fun, so enjoy! It is something that does not have to be an intensive process, and can be spread out over many months or a trip can be planned on the spur of the moment. Given that we often do not make hotel reservations, except for the last night of the trip, detailed planning is not necessary. You just need to do some training, plan your dates, chose your general route, get your air tickets, purchase guidebooks and maps, and the rest will come. Note the pre-trip checklist appendix to this book.

Here are some pre-trip tips:
- **Training:** Of course you should do some riding before the trip, but it is not necessary to prepare like you are going on the Tour de France! The more training you do, the relatively further you will be able to ride. But riding once or twice a week, even 20-25 miles per ride, for an 8 week period before your trip, can be enough for an

enjoyable tour. You will find that you will get stronger as the trip progresses, so the early days of a trip are often warm-up rides in any case.

- **Be Comfortable**: Ride enough that you are comfortable in your bike seat. That can be more important than huge miles of training. This is especially important if the trip is early in the season or you have a new seat. You will often be spending 4-8 hours on the bike per day, depending on your speed and route, so you need to be comfortable! Get a comfortable seat, not a racing seat.

- **Ride Some Hills**: Even if the trip is flat, do some hill training. There will be overpasses and other hills, especially if you ride from one river valley to another.

- **Map:** Get a good overall map of the area you are traveling to so you can be familiar with the entire route. Even if you have books that have maps of segments of the route, having one larger map with you can be useful.

- **Guide Books**: Purchase one or two general travel books that follow the route so you can use them for standard tourist information, like sites, hotels, and restaurant information. Don't be afraid to tear out the relevant sections, and leave the bulk of the book behind — don't carry more than you need. These books can also be downloaded to e-Readers for reduced weight and space.

- **Bikeline Books**: Purchase the relevant Bikeline books (published by Esterbauer) that cover your ride so you will have detailed directions and route information. Some of the books are only in German, while some are also in English. I have often used these German guides even thought I don't read German, and have had no problem since the important map key information is also in English, and consequently using the maps and directions is easy with only English. I have a section later in the book that shows how to use these books most effectively, even when written in German.

- **U.S. Tune-Up Rides**: There are many great rides in the U.S., but few routes that are not on roads and are of considerable distance. The Rails to Trails Conservancy is one of my favorite source of bike trails, but most routes are still short — but growing! But if you want to try a tour in the U.S. once before heading to Europe. Here are two routes to consider:

- o **C&O Canal Route**: From Cumberland, Maryland to Washington D.C., about 180 miles, not paved. This can also be extended by starting in Pittsburg, making the trip close to 350 miles. Many camp along this route, but it is possible to stay in hotels if you plan carefully.
- o **Erie Canal Route**: This route is about 400 miles from Buffalo, New York, to Albany, mostly paved or on lightly travelled routes. The Parks and Trails of New York (www.ptny.org) publishes an excellent route book, and also organizes rides in July each year.
- o Although both of these rides make fine experiences, neither will, in my opinion, provide the interesting, historic, cultural, and flexible features found when touring in Europe — but good tune-ups!

Logistics

How to Get You and Your Bike There

Getting from home to the start of a ride is not my favorite part of a trip, but there are ways to approach this logistic necessity to reduce cost, time, and inconvenience.

- **Bringing Bike**: I like bringing my own bike on a trip. The only reason I can think for not bringing your bike is if you don't want to have added complexity and cost of getting to and from your destination. But if this issue is managed, having your own bike can actually be less complicated and create less uncertainty than the alternatives.
- **Cost:** One issue for bringing your bike can be cost. Many airlines charge for bringing a bike, and some do not. This issue should be directly addressed when you are looking for international airfare. **Once you find your answer, make sure that this is documented in your flight record, so you don't have to deal with it again at check in.** These rules are always changing, and often even the airline officials at check-in are not up to date. So check this out carefully and document.
- **Packing the Bike:** If you are taking your bike, another question is how to package it for transport. I think that the fancy hard cases that require you to take much of the bike apart are a waste of time and energy unless you have a champion racing machine. I have taken my bike overseas for nearly two decades without damage in cardboard boxes. Originally I would put my bike in the cardboard boxes provided by the airlines, only taking off the pedals and leaving the panniers on as extra padding for the bike. I never had a problem. Now it is harder to get these boxes at the airport. A couple of years ago I was flying home from Berlin, and could not find a box anywhere in the airport. Luckily, I had several hours before the flight, so I went to the cargo section of the airport, found scrap shipping boxes, and fashioned a box around my bike. It worked great.
  - Note: Lufthansa Airways does not currently require that a bike even be placed in a bike box. The bike can be checked

in directly as is, with only the pedals removed. I would put some extra padding around the frame to prevent nicks, but this is an option, especially for an odd-sized bike, like a tandem. I did this recently with my tandem -- no problem. Make sure to contact the airline to confirm policies.

- **Bike Boxes**: I have used the mostly cardboard Aircaddy box for 5 years, without replacing it, and with no problem. (www.aircaddy.com). The box set (cardboard outer box and metal interior support system) is $99.95, but I also recommend the wheel and travel bag kits kit for another $80 so that the box can be more easily wheeled about. I simply remove the front wheel, put the bike in the box, and put my panniers and the front wheel in the empty area around the bike. Once you arrive in Europe, the box can be folded up into a nylon flat bag, which facilitates mailing it to other locations if you are flying in and out of different airports.
- **Multiple Airports**: Sometimes we like to fly into one airport and out from another. For example, on the Rhine Ride, you might like to fly into Amsterdam and home from Frankfurt. If you don't bring your own bike, this may not be practical since you would likely have to return your rented bike to the same location, meaning you would have to train back to your original airport at the end of the ride. To make use of two different airports, one for arrival and one for departure, we mail our bike boxes to the hotel we have reserved for the last night near our departure airport. These hotels are as close to our departing airport as we can reasonably find (some are right in the airport, like the Sheraton at Frankfurt Airport). With notice to these hotels, they have been fine accepting our mailed folded box and storing it until we get to the hotel many days later. We usually mail the knocked down box by standard postage service, often finding a post office in our arriving airport (check the airport website to see if they have a post office).
- **Airfare:** Airfare can be a significant part of the trip expense, even without paying any bike fees. Buying a roundtrip economy ticket to Europe can range from $700 to $1800 depending on timing and locations. I recommend booking as early as you can, especially if traveling during peak summer months. I often use frequent flyer

miles. If you save all year, charge everything, saving the required approximate 60,000 miles is feasible, especially if you take advantage of sign-up bonuses from credit cards. One nice thing about using miles is you can use them to come into one location and out from another, without additional cost. Again, book ahead. For example, United typically allows you to book using miles 330 days ahead of your trip.

- **Arrival:** Once you arrive at the airport you might end up riding right out the front door, as we have done many times, or taking a train to your starting point. More on trains later, but it is good to do research on this before you leave home. Once you arrive take advantage of the information desks at the airport that can help with trains and other local logistic questions (such as what is the riding route out of that airport). The information desk staff almost always speak English. If we are flying in and out of the same airport, we find a hotel near the airport, reserve it ahead of time, and then take our folded boxes (walking, taxi, shuttle) to the hotel when we arrive and they store the boxes until the end of the trip.

- **Summary Trip Process**: Here is a summary process I use to handle all the issues discussed above:
    - Determine route.
    - Purchase airfare, either roundtrip into the same airport, or into one airport and out from another.
    - Reserve a hotel for the last night of the trip near the departing airport.
    - Purchase Bikeline Books and other guidebooks.
    - Use the checklist in the Appendix to collect all you need for the trip.
    - A week before the ride, pack up the bike to give time to make sure everything is fine and nothing forgotten -- and not taking too much!
    - On the day of departure, get to the airport early. I like to get there at least 3 hours early just so there is time to handle any uncertainty. TSA, and its international counterparts, can take time, and some check-in agents are less familiar with bikes than others (again, put what you find about fares in your record.)

- After check-in you will often have to take your bike to the TSA station. You cannot touch anything during their inspection process, but by being there you are ready for any questions, and you can politely ask the officer to re-tape the box in a sturdy fashion.
- I carry onboard my back rack bag or handle bar bag.
- Upon arrival at your destination go to the oversize area of the luggage claim.
- Get your bike and find a corner of the luggage area inside customs where there is not much traffic, to unpack, set the bike up, and fold up your box. I also change into bike clothes in the restrooms which are normally nearby. (This process typically takes about 30 minutes.)
- Wheel the bikes and the folded box out through customs (I never had a problem with that), and go to the airport information desk. Find out where the post office is, if you need it, and also any train schedules that you need to confirm. You can also ask if there is a route for riding right out of the airport, if that is your plan.
- Have one person take the bike boxes to your nearby hotel that you reserved for the last night of your trip, or mail the boxes at airport— the other can watch the bikes.
- Start your ride (usually before 10 in the morning in Europe), or head to the train station to get to your starting point.
- Have a great trip!
- At the end of the trip, the day before you fly home, get to your reserved hotel near your departure airport. In some cases you can ride from the river right to the airport.
- Collect your bike box from the hotel, and pack up your bike the night before departure. Leave the packed bike in your hotel room or in a storage room (or sometimes we use the hotel's smaller meeting rooms where we can lock the door.)
- Arrange transport for the morning of the flight in a hotel van or large taxi, if necessary, and plan to get to the airport 3 hours ahead.

- o Take your back rack or handle bar bag with you on your flight home.
- o Have a safe trip home!

How to Get Around: Trains and Boats and Other Sag Wagons

Trains, and to a lesser degree, boats, are a key part of the logistical support system for each ride. Here are a few tips:

- **To Start Ride**: We often use trains to get to our starting point on the ride, or from the end point of the ride back to our departing airport.
- **Skip Segments**: Trains can be used during the trip to skip a segment of the route. For example, on the northern Rhine route you might want to skip an industrial segment near the Saar to leave time for more scenic areas. We once took a train in this area for about 60 miles, taking just a bit more than an hour, but saving a day of riding for a higher priority segment. Don't think you are cheating by skipping a section, you are just employing smart time management!
- **Finish a Day:** Trains can be used during a day to get from the end of a day's ride to the city where you want to spend the night. For example, you might have finished 40 miles by 2:30 in the afternoon, and then can take a train 20 miles to an interesting city so you can get there with time to explore. This might provide for a more attractive opportunity than simply sleeping in the town you rode to before boarding the train.
- **Equalize Riders**: Trains can be used to help equalize riders. Some riders might like to do more miles than others. Groups can ride together until a certain time of the day, and then some can train to the destination and others can complete the ride. This also works with some riders leaving early in the day, and others catching up mid-morning using trains.
- **Special Bike Trains**:
  - o Not all trains allow bikes onboard.
  - o This is especially true for high-speed trains. Even some local trains require reservations for bikes, and these

reservations can be obtained at the ticket offices in train stations.

o The cost of a ticket is for the passenger, and normally an additional ticket is required for the bike. Don't forget the bike ticket, there can be fines if you don't have one with you.

o Look for the train car with a bike painted on the side, these are designed for bikes. Most often they are in the rear of the train. Some stations also have guides posted telling where the bike cars will stop. Often you don't have much time to get aboard, since trains can stop for only a few minutes — you need to race to the right spot and get onboard quickly.

- **Find Routes Ahead**: Various national rail systems have websites so you can check routes and bike trains ahead of time. Here is the link for Germany, for example:

  http://www.bahn.de/i/view/USA/en/index.shtml.

- **Boats/Ships.** River boats can play a similar role to trains — only more scenic! There are several sections of various routes that are especially tourist-friendly, and have tour boats that run during the season. These boats almost always allow bikes onboard, and make a great break during the day:

  o To reduce mileage for a day.

  o To provide a chance to see the scenery from the perspective of being on the river, rather than beside the river.

  o To take a break.

  o To have a meal or snack while cruising, with most boats having restaurants that serve surprisingly good food.

  o To see scenery such as certain gorges, for example, where bikes just cannot go.

  o Here are some boat companies—**this is actually very valuable information, make sure to print out schedules from the applicable websites before your trip**:

- **Rhine:**
  - www.k-d.com.
  - www.loreley-linie.de.
  - www.bingen-ruedesheimer.de.
- **Rhine and Neckar:**
  - www.rnf-schifffahrt.de.
- **Mosel:**
  - www.moselfahrplan.de.
- **Elbe:**
  - http://www.saechsische-dampfschiffahrt.de.
- **Weser:**
  - www.hal-oever.de.
  - www.weserschiff-linie2000.de.
  - www.flotte-wesser.de.
- **Danube:**
  - www.schiffahrt-kelheim.de.
  - www.donauschiffahrt.de.
  - www.brandner.at.
  - www.donauschiffahrt-wurm.de.

Typical Tour Boat on Rhine

- **Ferries**. In many places routes will take you across the river not by bridge, but by other interesting methods. This includes the use of many smaller and larger ferries. These ferries are marked on the Bikeline maps.
    - Note: Most of the time these are operational, but sometimes, especially on quieter stretches, they are not operational.
    - Tip: Keep Euro coins ready for the short ferry rides, usually 1 to 2 Euros per person including bikes.

Michael J. Lyon

Larger Ferry

Smaller Ferry

- **Other Crossings**: Another interesting way to get across certain rivers is by walking across walkways on top of hydroelectric dams. These dams do not serve as bridges for cars, but often bikes and riders can cross. It can be a challenge carrying a bike and load up the steps that are often encountered, but then there is the view!

- **Luggage and Route Facilitators:** One alternative to consider for logistics are the European companies that will assist you with your trip, without serving as full trip operators. They will often move your luggage from overnight location to location, provide general route information, make hotel reservations, and provide a customer service feature. They sometimes provide guides, but also facilitate self-guided touring. In some ways, this option represents something between going on your own, as is mainly outlined in this book, and going on a formal guided tour. Some of these services even offer sag wagon features in addition to luggage moving.
  - o **Tip**: This might be a good alternative for riders who want to avoid having to carry luggage on rides. The downside is this approach provides less flexibility, and does come with an added, albeit not extreme, added cost.
  - o See the following as examples of some of these services:
    - www.radurlaub.com.
    - www.eruobike.at.
    - www.oesterreich-radreisen.at.

- Note: I cannot recommend any particular one of these companies since I have never used any of these types of firms.

Navigation Hints: GPS, Compass, Maps

Navigating during the ride is not as difficult as one would expect, and much easier and less stressful than it used to be when I started touring. Thank you GPS! But in addition to this high-tech tool, the oldest marker around is also a great navigational guide — the river itself. In many cases you stay within sight of the river, and rarely travel more than a mile or two from its banks.

- **GPS**: Consider bringing along a GPS. I have a Garmin 705, which is terrific. I rode for many years with only a compass, and that worked just fine, but a GPS makes it easy. The Garmin also allows me to upload maps of the region I am touring, so I always know where I am and can find distances and detours easily.
  - o **Tip**: Since njmost of these routes are on bike trails rather than roads, you don't want to use the typical road navigation function in the GPS. Rather, find and enter as waypoints 8-12 cities along a day's route, and use these as waypoints for the day's ride. That way the 705 can be set up so that an arrow always points toward the next target and gives distance. If you get more than 30-40 degrees off target, stop and see if you're headed down the wrong path or road. The GPS also comes in handy locating a particular hotel, restaurant, or attraction in a city. Note that the newer Gamin Bike GPS does not currently have this arrow function, so check carefully.
- **Compass**. I always also carry a compass. It is a good backup. One approach is a Casio triple sensor watch with compass. These watches will also give you some sense of weather (barometric pressure) and altitude. The compass can also be handy when you are off the bike, walking around a town, and don't have your GPS with you.
- **Maps**: Bring a good map of the area, and the appropriate Bikeline books covering your ride.

Where to Stay, Eat, and How Much Will it Cost

Accommodations: Hotel, Camping, Reservations

There are many ways to approach the accommodation process — low cost, high-end, camping, reservations, no reservations, and other issues. Here are a few thoughts:

- **Camping?**: Camping or not camping is a fundamental question you need to address. If you camp you will need to carry much more with you on your bike, and will likely travel a relatively shorter distance with a comparative amount of physical effort. If you are in great shape and don't mind being fully loaded with front and rear panniers, camping is certainly an option. However, I have never camped, and never missed it. If I want to camp, I will do that on a hiking trip. When biking, I want to travel as light as I can, and I enjoy the simple comforts of a bed and warm shower in a private bath at the end of a long day. Therefore, the bulk of my comments focus on staying in hotels. But here is a bit more on camping:
    - Advantages:
        - A major advantage of camping is reduced cost vs. a hotel room.
        - Gives you more time outside, and a bit more of an "adventure."
        - Can often sleep in very beautiful locations, with many campgrounds located along the rivers.
        - More likely to eat dinner in simple locations or cook, a different experience and less costly.
        - Almost always room at a campsite.
    - Disadvantages:
        - A downside is you will likely need to carry as much as double what you would need to take without camping. So heavier load, less easy and comfortable trip. If need to carry the load, consider a trailer, like the Bob Yak Plus

trailer, easier than a large load on the bike, and given the flat routes in this books, less problematic.

- It is also more difficult to stay in the middle of cities if camping since campgrounds are often outside of towns. This is another major negative from my perspective.
- Less good restaurants and less variety for dinner.
- More exposed to bad weather — no place to get out of raining weather and dry off.

- **Hotel Priorities**: Hotels in Europe can vary from one-star simple rooms, to five-star world-class accommodations. What you chose is largely based on your budget. For the budget we target, about $110 or $140 per day total (single occupancy), we generally stay in 2- or 3-star hotels. The features we look for include:
  - Private bathroom.
  - No smoking room.
  - A secure place to leave our bikes, either in the room, or more likely in a shed or storage room that can be locked.
  - Convenient location so we can walk to the places we want to visit that day, and not get back on the bikes.
  - Hair dryer is a plus, especially if you are washing clothes that night and want a Plan B if they don't dry overnight naturally.
  - Sometimes we choose chains, like Ibis or Motel One in Germany, where you know what you are going to get, nothing interesting, but dependable. These are especially good options in larger, more expensive, cities, where other options can be more costly.
- **Booking Offices**: Sometimes it is useful to use the tourist office in various cities when you arrive for help finding a room. This can be better than riding from place to place if the town is crowded — let them call around for you, usually at little or no cost. These offices can also help you book a day or two ahead for your next destinations, once you know your route for the next day or two.

- **Nicer Hotels Sometimes**: A few times per trip we splurge for a nicer place. This generally happens if:
    - There is a special historic hotel in the area, such as a converted castle or monastery that is now a hotel.
    - Something with great views or very special location.
    - There is nothing else in town, especially in larger towns where even simple hotels can cost more.
    - Many of the hotels recommended in the book are slightly over budget, but are otherwise worth consideration.
- **To Reserve or Not Reserve**: A key issue to consider is whether to reserve or not reserve hotels for your trip ahead of time. We always reserve the last night of the trip, especially since these hotels might be storing our bike boxes. We never reserve other nights, except a day or two ahead sometimes, or when we are targeting a specific hotel that we don't want to miss. Some might think this is just too risky or unstructured — but it has worked well for us for many years with very few close calls. **Should consider reserving if there is an event in the town (conference, wine festival, etc.) and Saturday nights a couple of days ahead. Also consider reservations around busy Lake Bodensee.**
  There are pluses and minuses with this approach, as compared to reserving rooms for your trip ahead of time.
    - **Advantages:**
        - Flexibility day-by-day on the route. You can stop when tired, go further if you like, or stop when you find something interesting and just want to stay longer.
        - More flexibility regarding weather, allowing you to deal with rainy days, for example. If you had made reservations for an entire trip, it would be difficult to spend an extra night in a town going to museums on a day with unusually miserable weather.
        - Ability to find a special place to stay in town— you can see something you like and go for it.
        - The ability to get better last minute deals.
        - You don't need to do as much planning ahead since you don't need to reserve hotels along the route and determine exact riding distances.

- You can reduce risk by riding not too late into the day, or even calling ahead for a hotel that morning or early afternoon.
  - **Disadvantages:**
    - More uncertainty about finding a room.
    - Especially problematic if you are riding during the core of the European summer vacation period (mid-July to late-August).
    - Occasional inability to stay in a particular hotel that might be fully booked.
    - Harder to ride late in the day and get a good room, arriving in town after 5:00 can be tougher.
  - **Conclusion:** The bottom-line is we have been riding without reservations for nearly two decades and have not had problems, and enjoy the flexibility this approach delivers. We have never found ourselves without a place to say. If you don't appreciate that flexibility compared to certainty, reserve ahead — but keep in mind the downsides of this approach.

Eating

Eating on trips is one of my special pleasures— more good food, less guilt. I especially enjoy stops at European bakeries and a choice of things you might only find in the fanciest establishments in America.

- **Breakfast**: Breakfast usually comes with your room. These breakfasts are typically simple in the level of hotels we stay in, but get progressively better with more expensive hotels. A 3-Star hotel will generally have coffee/tea, juice, rolls/bread, cheese, sliced salami, hard boil egg, and cereal.

Typical German Hotel Breakfast

- **Lunch**: Lunch is usually on the road, in an attractive location that we discover, or one that is just convenient. Often we will find a restaurant along the river with nice views. But sometimes there is just not much out there and you are happy with whatever you find. One of the good standbys can be the Turkish Doner Kebab/Pizza places in many towns, a good buy.

- **Breaks**: We usually take breaks every 10-15 miles for a snack in between meals. But we also carry a few "emergency" rations — a hunk of cheese, or one of the "power" bars. We rarely need these, but they are good to have in case you are on a longer stretch without a food stop. As you can see from these pictures, pastries and snacks can be fantastic in Europe. Another nice break can be wineries and wine stands, which are often found in the river areas — there are many vineyards along rivers.

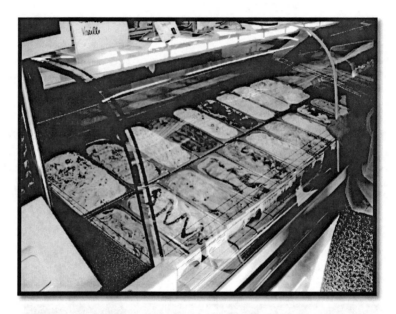

- **Dinner**: Dinner is usually a highlight of the day, well deserved after many miles. And we eat quite well, even within our budget. Dinner can be at a scenic perch along the river, a historic venue, or even in the hotel. Many European hotels, even smaller ones, have excellent restaurants owned and operated by a family. Don't think Holiday Inn Route 95 restaurants. We also like the historic restaurants. Note: Beer or a glass of local wine can be as inexpensive as a Coke or bottled water, but if you drink a lot, you might break the budget provided as our norm!

600 Year-Old Bremen Ratskeller — UNESCO World Heritage

Budget

So how much will all this cost? You may be surprised just how inexpensive these trips can be — yet comfortable. We never feel like we are skimping. The bottom-line is you don't need to spend a fortune to have a first-class European cycling adventure.

- **Budget Per-Day**: Our overall average per day budget is $110-140 per day. Note that riding in Switzerland will increase expenses.
- **Hotels:**
  - o We stay in hotels with our own in-suite bathrooms. This can cost a bit more than sharing a bathroom, but is a nice way to travel. It also makes doing your laundry easier!
  - o There is a misconception on the relative cost of European accommodations. They can be expensive, but for purposes of this book and the types of trips recommended, they are usually cheaper than one would find in the United States for similar lodging. We tend to budget $45-$80 per night for a single hotel room, although in some larger towns we might spend as much as $100 per night or more. If you can share a room, your cost will be less. There are also chains, like IBIS, that provide standardized rooms between 59-79 Euros. Finally, when we find a special hotel, something historic, like a converted castle or monastery, or something else that makes the hotel more than just a place to sleep, we will spend more. We usually do that a few nights per trip.
- **Meals:**
  - o Rooms come with breakfast, so one meal is already included in this cost!
  - o Lunch usually costs $8-15 per day, and dinner can be as much as $35 in a nicer establishment.
- **Local Transport**: We will often take one train ride of 2-3 hours as part of the route, and this can cost about $20 to $40 with bikes (you need a special bike ticket). Shorter train rides, such as to skip a section of a ride, are generally $8-15.

What to Bring: The Bike and What Goes On It

The primary idea here is bring as little as possible, just what you need, and nothing more. This is not an easy balance, but here less is more. Keep in mind that in many cases you are not riding in the middle of nowhere, and supplies and bike parts can be found in many locations. I have repaired my bike on several occasions during the ride, even relatively major issues, such as a new derailleur, and have found the shops as good or better than what I find at home.

What Type of Bike

This of course is a key issue. If you have decided to bring your own bike, now the question is what kind of bike to bring: road, touring, mountain, hybrid, tandem?

- **Road Bikes**: I am not a fan of standard road bikes for touring. I just don't think they are strong enough for these types of trips. They are built for speed, not durability, generally. Many will work, but I have also seen many not make it. The tire width and wheel rims are especially problematic, since routes will often have segments on gravel or worse for stretches. Thinner tires are also less stable with load, and can be more dangerous with wet or slippery roads. I know many people like touring with these bikes, they are faster, but I go for strength and stability.
- **Touring Bikes**: On the other hand, a good touring road bike, with strong rims, at least 21 gears, and wider tires, can be a good choice. I like tires that are on the wider side:700-32 or 700-35 tire. Take a look at the Schwalbe Marathon Plus 700c, as an example, although there are faster options, as well.
  - o Recommendation: One 700c bike that I like is the Bruce Gordon Rock N' Road Tour. Strong, good quality and can have wider tires for the off-road patches that can come on these routes. My Uncle has been using his for 30 years, and it has worked quite well.
- **Mountain Bike or Hybrid**: My first choice for touring is not a bike many might consider: a lightweight mountain bike with lockable

front shocks and high-pressure slick tires. I have been touring with this arrangement all these years. I like 1.25 inch slick tires with 90 psi. These are fast and stable. The front (lockable) shock will help on bumpy trails and make the trip more comfortable, but rear shocks are not necessary and often will not work with many panniers. I would also pick a bike that is less than 30 pounds without load. My mountain bike is 24 pounds. I want something strong, with good rims, but not too heavy. A nice hybrid could also work well. A cheaper bike will often be too heavy, and not reliable enough for these trips. I tend to think that a bike for these trips should cost at least $500, as a rule of thumb, although a good bargain might work.

- **Tandems:** Another option is taking a tandem. This can be a good option for couples and families, especially if the riders are of different strength — it can allow for longer rides together. I have started touring with my 8-year-old son using a German tandem, the Hase Pino (made for adults and children), which allows my son to be seated in front with seat belt, and I am in back steering.

Cycling Along Europe's Rivers

- **Frame Material:** I like steel frames for touring, strong and comfortable. Aluminum is another choice, lightweight and fine especially if you have a shock absorber since aluminum can be a stiffer ride. I tend to stay away from carbon given that these frames are easier to damage during shipping and can be an expensive target for theft. Titanium is great, but expensive and might also cause more security concerns.

- **Comfortable**: A very important issue is being comfortable on your bike. Make sure you spend time on it before the trip. Find a good seat. Consider positioning the handle bars so you can sit up a bit more than you might for day riding. It is not necessary to lean over all the time in a racing position; this can be tough if you ride for many hours every day.

- **Wheels:** Make sure you have strong rims, especially your rear rim, no matter what type of bike you have. The rear wheels should be stronger than standard wheels if possible, and checked carefully by your mechanic before departure, together with spokes.

- **Tune-Up**: Get a good tune up before you leave. I always get new tires, new tubes, and a new chain and cassette every year even if the existing components are not that worn. Don't listen to your mechanic who says this is unnecessary — just get these items! It is just not worth having a flat in the middle of nowhere, or breaking a chain.(I have experienced both problems before moving to this policy, and not since.)

- **Rental Bikes**: It can be possible to rent a bike in Europe if you are flying in and out from the same airport. As mentioned, I like bringing my bike, but renting a bike is certainly an option to limit airport hassles and airline bike fees. Search the web and contact a few shops ahead of time. Reserve your bike and put down a deposit, if necessary. Request something dependable and good quality. Consider bringing your own seat so you will feel a bit more at home. The Lake Bodensee ride is well-suited to renting a local bike.

- **Conclusion:** Make sure your bike has tires that are not too thin, is not too heavy, and is well-built—something you are comfortable riding.

Packed Equipment

My mantra: Take what you need and no more. If riding with others, divide up equipment that can be shared to avoid duplications.

- Bike pump (small).
- GPS, if you can, and a compass.
- General multi-component tool with screwdriver, hex wrenches.
- Tire changing tool and chain tool (optional).
- Tape, one electric tape role for small repairs, and one packing roll for taping box up upon your departure (keep that roll with your bike box).
- Bike bell, required in Germany, for example.
- Two extra tubes.
- Small first-aid kit, including Band-Aids, benadryl for bites, and triple antibiotic cream. Consider bringing a general oral antibiotic in case of infection.
- Camera.
- Phone that has international roaming turned on (GSM). This is really not a luxury anymore, but something you must bring. Every rider should have a working phone. This is the best way to find someone if you get separated, which can happen! It also helps if you split up during a day, such as if one person takes a train to the next town ahead of others. It is also possible to purchase a local SIM card for your unlocked phone, or buy an inexpensive local phone, to make calling cheaper. If you are going to be doing a lot of calls during the day, this is a good option. Otherwise, Skype works well when you have Wi-Fi, such at the end of the ride in your hotel or at a local coffee shop.
- I like traveling with my iTouch these days, providing all my reading and entertainment on a small, light, device. I also use the Wi-Fi feature to do Skype calling from my hotel, with most having free Wi-Fi these days. iPhones and Android devices will also play this role. I have considered bringing a small tablet, but so far have resisted having one more large expensive thing to worry about.
- Chargers with small plug adapters. You don't need electric current adapters, just the small plug adapters – don't take more than you need.

- Suntan lotion.
- One lock per bike.

Clothes

We don't like to do major laundry on our trips, but do small washes in the sink. We don't pack for style, but for flexibility and to be able to carry a small load of drip dry clothing where possible. Here are some recommendations:

- Two riding shirts. We always ride with the yellow shirts these days. A bit boring, but easy to see in low light, and easy to find others in your group. Drip-dry. I wash these and the shorts every other day in my hotel sink, especially if I have a hair dryer in the room.
- One pair of riding shorts. These can also be used as swim wear, but you can also bring a bathing suit.
- One pair of riding shoes. I do not recommend clip in pedals and shoes, just too much off and on in this type of riding.
- One pair of shoes for off-bike and three pair of off-bike socks. You can get away with only the one pair of shoes, but it is great to have an alternative. Find something lightweight. Some like sandals, but they are not great if it is rainy or cold, so I like full-toed shoes.
- Underwear and riding socks for each day. Thin socks take less packing space. Many ride with less, but I prefer not to have to wash these during a ride given drying time.
- One lightweight raincoat, with vents, made for example with Gortex.
- One thin fleece sweater/sweatshirt. I like fleece since it can be packed into a very small space when compressed in the plastic bag system described later.
- One long-sleeve shirt, drip dry.
- One or two drip dry short-sleeve shirts for off the bike.
- One pair of long pants, drip dry, and with zip off bottoms to provide extra use flexibility.
- One pair of lightweight shorts.
- One hat.
- One or Two tee shirts.

- Of course, this is focused on what a man would bring, and would need to be adjusted somewhat for a women!
- The key is bring only what you need, what can be washed in the sink, dries quickly, folds up easily, non-wrinkle, and flexible enough for a variety of circumstances— warm or cooler, dry or wet, using layering and multiple combinations.

How To Pack

Here are some pointers that make packing easier:
- Get larger zip lock bags (2.5 gallons), with the slide locks. I usually take about 10-12 for a ride.
- Use one bag for each side compartment of your panniers, and several for the central compartment.
- Roll up clothes tightly, and place in a bag based on type. Underwear in one, off bike clothes in another, and so on.
- Once the bag is full, squeeze the air out and zip it closed in its compressed configuration.
- This approach has the following advantages:
  o This makes everything waterproof— what kind of pannier you have regarding waterproofing matters very little in this case.
  o By squeezing all the air out, the package can be compressed, taking up a minimum amount of space in your pannier.
  o It is easy to find your clothes once separated into different bags. I even have a bag for laundry.

Panniers

With the packing style outlined above, the quality of the pannier is less important:
- **Waterproof**: Unless you are camping, I would not go for the heavy waterproof panniers. Not necessary and too heavy. They also tend to have less outside pockets. But I would protect your panniers with waterproof spray before the ride. The German's swear by the Ortlieb Panniers, but not my preference given my zip lock approach.

- **Type**: Panniers come in all sizes and price ranges. My favorite is the GT-54 by Arkel, expensive, but considerable space and flexibility. But this is the high end, and especially if you are just getting started, these are not necessary. Also, these types of stronger bags are heavier, so there are negatives to this kind of choice.
- **Must Fit Bike**: Make sure the panniers fit your bike, are easy to put on and take off, and don't come off when you are riding even on bumpy roads. This sounds obvious, but I have been with too many riders who keep losing their bags when going over a big bump! You might consider a couple of bungee cords just in case the bags start slipping.
- **Rear Only**: If you are not camping, only large rear panniers are necessary if you pack light. Having front panniers just makes riding more complicated and are not necessary.
- **Pockets:** Having a few outside pockets is nice so that the whole bag does not need to be opened every time. It is also a plus to have a bag that has a zip-off side pouch that can be taken with you when off the bike with your valuables (wallet, camera, GPS, passport, phone). We often leave our panniers unguarded during a mid-day sightseeing excursion. We lock up the bikes, and do take valuables with us. We have not had a problem with this approach.
- **Handle Bar or Rear Bag**: It is also useful to have one extra bag, either a handle bar bag, or a rear rack bag. This provides space for things used often, and can be taken off the bike for a hike if needed. It is also something that can be carried on the plane for your transatlantic flights.

Guide Books

Bikeline (Esterbauer)Books

A central component of the type of touring discussed in this book is having a detailed set of maps that supports the trip. The Bikeline collection of books is excellent — and all the rides in this book are based on this series. These books have the following advantages and features:

- **Detailed Maps:** These books provide detailed maps of the entire route, with detail that actually displays each building along the route in many cases. Other types of books that give you routes, even turn-by-turn information, are less useful than having the detailed maps provided in this series. This is especially true given GPS.

- **Topographic Information:** The books provide topographical information that lets you know which routes have hills, and where the hills come during the ride. This allows you to ride the hills, if you like, or find ways to avoid especially hilly sections, such as taking trains or boats during those stretches.

- **City Maps:** Many key cities along the routes, usually the major or most interesting cities in that area, have more detailed city-level map inserts, in addition to route information.

- **Tested and Updated**: The routes have been tested by actual people riding these routes, and updated on a regular basis. On average, routes are updated every two years or less.

- **Language Issues:** Many of the books are in German, with English being added for certain popular routes such as the Danube and the Elbe rivers. But you don't need to read German to use all the books— I don't. The legend in the front of these books is also in English, meaning that all the maps and various symbols can be understood. What you do miss if you don't read German is the discussions about individual cities. I make up for this by getting standard English language guidebooks.

- **Additional Information:** The series also has lists of hotels along the route in the back of each book, and even in German, this section can be used by English readers for phone numbers of hotels at various locations, and also to judge how many hotels are in an upcoming city and determine where to stop. You don't want to plan to end at 5 pm in a city that turns out not to have any hotels!

- **Useful Format:** The books have a landscape orientation and spiral binding that makes them easy to use, and can be placed in handlebar holders if so desired. While all the books are fairly durable, some editions have plastic laminated pages, indicated by a "wetterfestreissfest" symbol.
- **How to Buy**: It can be challenging to purchase the books outside of Europe. Please see the following website for current information on purchasing these books:
www.cycletouringbooks.com.
- **Website**: Esterbauer has an excellent website that can provide you with current information about books and routes, including allowing the user to explore each book in a summary fashion to identify distances, basic route information, and elevation changes (a key factor when determining where to ride). One hint is use Google translate to read the website, it works reasonably well.
www.esterbauer.com.

Using Bikeline Books

Even in German, utilizing the maps of these books is easy given that that the legend is in German and English. Turn to the Kartenlegende page in each book. You will find a scale, typically 15 km per page. You will also find a key that shows a few of the most important features. Here are some examples:

- o Solid red lines are the main cycle routes. You will want to ride on these routes where possible.
- o Solid green lines are also bike routes and usually quite good.
- o If the red or green lines have large dashes, the path is unpaved. The condition can vary, but if you have good tires (not racing road bike tires) you should have no

problem. You might also appreciate the front shock on your bike during these sections.

o   If the red or green lines have small dashes, this is a rough road. Some riders might prefer to ride on a nearby road rather than these trails, it just depends on how bumpy a ride you can handle and how busy the alternative street. If there is a long segment like this, and not good road alternative, consider a boat or train to skip that section.

o   A line with dots means the route for this section is actually on a road. I would advise staying off the yellow lines with red dots unless there is no choice. A yellow line with green dots is fine, since that usually means a bike shoulder or an adjacent bike trail.

o   Along the maps you will see lines that look like pins sticking out from the route, at about a 70 degree angle, and numbers in red between two of these pins. This indicates the distance between the pins in kilometers.

o   A bed in a blue box indicates a hotel or guesthouse, indicating a town that you can spend the night.

o   A plate with utensils is a place to stop for a meal or snack.

o   Castles and churches are indicated, as well as museums.

o   A small boat can be an important symbol, indicating a ferry for crossing the river.

o   A rail line going into a town can be important, and look for the small dot or box on the rail line indicating a station (Bahnhof) – important if you want to skip a section and are looking for the next train stop.

o   Arrows on the route indicate uphill or downhill, watch these to avoid long hills if possible.

- **Sample Map Pages**: The following are a few map pages from the Bikeline books and a brief explanation on how to best use these maps:

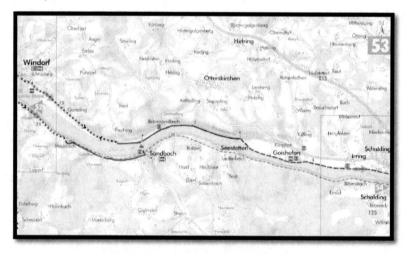

  - This is map 53 of the route. This will correlate to the large summary map for the route, which is shown for each of the recommended books inside the front cover.
  - Map 52 overlaps on the west, or left of the book, with lines showing where it overlaps. For example, Windorf is

found in both Map 52 and Map53.The same for Scholding, found in Map53 and Map 54.

o The Danube flows the direction of the arrow in the river, that is, from west to east.

o From about Windorf to Sandbach, the route is on both sides of the river. On the south side, east of Hausbach, the route is a cycle route with moderate motor traffic. There is no bike path here, but a small road for riding and some traffic. On the north side, from Windorf to near Fisching, there is a bike path alongside a road. Note the arrows facing each other — indicating there is a hill on this stretch.

o From near Fisching to across the river from Seetetten, the path is a main cycle route, and likely a nice ride along the river. Also, between the pins that start along that path, from the boat image to where the solid green line turns to dashed green line, there is a "3", indicating that distance is 3 km between the pins.

o Across the river from Seestetten, on the north side of the river, the green lines turns to dashes, meaning this is an unpaved road.

o At Sandbach, there is a ferry across the river, allowing you to change sides of the river, and cross from south to north side if you are not already on the north side.

o At Gaishofen, note there is both lodging and food available. You could also find lodging and food at Sandbach.

o Note the rail line on the south side of river. Near Laufenbach there is a box on the rail line, indicating a station at that location.

o Note the little dots on the maps, especially around cities. These are actually all the buildings in that area — that is the level of detail on these maps!

• The following are two maps covering the same area, but with routes on both sides of the river.

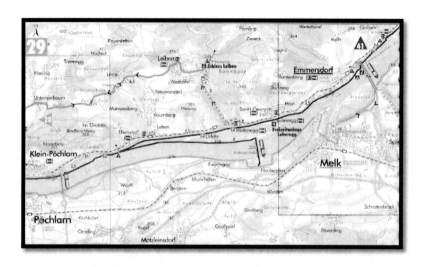

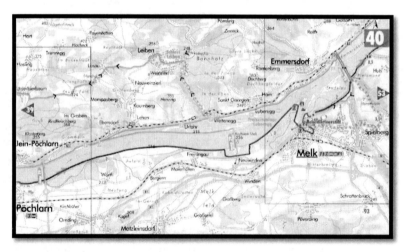

- Note how these map number pages are different colors, indicating there are two routes covered.
- When there are two routes, there are often crossing places between the routes. I advise studying the routes the night before to look at surfaces (do you want to ride on roads, avoid hills, see certain cities) and determine which side to ride.
- On Map 29, there are three crossings: a bridge near Pochlarn, a Bridge just east of Emmersdorf, and a dam near Newwinden. This

is one of the dams that can be crossed by bike, but often requires climbing some stairs.

- On the north side, there are two routes shown: one that takes you to Schloss Leiben, a castle, taking you away from the river and requiring some climbing. There is also a nice bike route (green) along the river and providing a crossing on the dam so that Melk can be visited.
- You can tell Melk is a bigger town by the number of buildings (dots) shown.
- Map 40 also shows that there is a good green path on the south side of the river, which looks like a good, simple ride with your river on your left. It would take you right into Melk.
- Upon exiting Melk, you would have the choice of crossing the river and taking the north side (which is what I would do here), or staying on the south side of the river.

Standard Travel Guides

Standard guide books are also important to provide information on hotels, sites, restaurants, and other logistic information. Therefore, it is important to bring along standard general travel books for your trip. For example, look for books like *Frommer's*, *Fodor's*, *Rick Steves*, or *Lonely Planet*.

- **History and Context**: These books can give you information about the history and cities that you are riding through. This is especially important when you are using Bikeline books in German. But I like having these types of books even when Bikeline books are in English.
- **At least two books**. I like to buy two guide books for the area I am riding, in addition to the Bikeline books. But don't bring the entire books. Tear them apart! Take only the sections that are relevant. I know that destroying a book is not something everyone is comfortable with, but don't take more than you need. (Of course, never tear up this book! Just copy the pages you need and bring them along.)

- **Download Versions**: One useful approach is to download the books to your iTouch, iPad, phone, or other e-Reader. That allows you to have several books with you, and no added weight or space utilized.

- **Recommendations:** Books like Frommer's and Rick Steves have recommendations on sites, restaurants, and hotels. I usually look at those 2-3 days ahead of a city to help identify special hotel experiences, such as castles or other more unique hotels, and reserve ahead if we can predict schedules and we think what is offered is worth the generally higher price than our standard 2- or 3-star hotels. These can often be memorable stops, and a good way to allocate limited funds, on occasion. The recommendations can also help fine-tune stops at sites along the route, or meal stops.

Safety and Security, Communication

Staying safe and protecting your property should always be a priority on a ride.

Safety

- **Bright Color Clothing**: Wear bright colors on the road. Bright yellow jerseys are recommended. Don't forget the raincoats—probably the most important garment that needs to be a bright color since you will often use these coats in lower light situations.
- **Head and Hands**: Helmets and gloves, of course.
- **Lights**: Flashing lights on the rear are especially important if you ride early or late, or when you are on a road.
- **Evacuation Insurance**: It is not a bad idea to purchase an emergency medical evacuation policy. Healthcare in Europe is usually quite good, often better than in the U.S., so this is not always necessary. On the other hand, if something happens, you will likely want to get home as quickly as you can, and these policies can help. I have found MedjetAssist (www.medjetassist.com) to provide reasonable flexibility.

Security

- **Locks**: Each rider should have a lock, and lock up their bike at each stop and in the evening. There is no easy way to lock up the panniers when you take a break away from your bike during the day, but take your valuables with you. Look for a place to leave your bike if you want to explore a castle or museum, such as at the restaurant where you just ate lunch.
- **Passport**: Keep your passport especially safe. Keep a photo copy of your passport in your wallet just in case.
- **Cash**: Don't carry large amounts of cash, use ATMs, which are almost everywhere now.

Staying in Touch

Another aspect of safety and security, as well as something you may just want to do, is finding ways to communicate back home.

- **International Phone**: As mentioned, bring a GSM phone with international roaming, or buy an inexpensive local phone and a local SIM card.
- **Wi-Fi**: One of the great developments is VOIP calling, using local Wi-Fi in hotels or other locations. Many phones will allow you to turn off your network, and make calls using Wi-Fi over Skype apps or other approaches. I have also used my iTouch and smart phone this way.
- **Emails:** With some phone systems, checking email is not that expensive, for example Blackberry, even when overseas. Other systems can be quite expensive. Last year I had my fancy Android phone turned on in London for 3 days, hardly used it, but had hundreds of dollars of data charges. Be careful! tend to check emails using my iTouch in the hotel using Wi-Fi connections. But if you need to check more than at night, find other solutions.
- **Texting:** Texting can be a great way to communicate, since this is often not too expensive, even when overseas. Check with your carrier.
- **Phone Photo**: Sending photos from your phone can also be a great way to share the moment with friends and family back home.
- **Computers**: Many hotels have computers you can use, and there can be other locations in town. Use them for email or Skype. Some riders even use them to maintain a daily blog on their trip. I have never taken my own computer, but that is a possibility. Consider an iPad if you need to be able to work while traveling.

Where and When to Go

There are many factors to consider when deciding on a route. We have discussed some of them above, including terrain and the quality of the supporting infrastructure.

Countries

A fundamental question when planning is determining which country you would like to ride. Most of our routes are in Germany and other near-by countries. That is generally because Germany has many great rides and a river network.

Germany

- o Germany is at the core of many of the rides in this book because Germany just has so many great trails.
  - Easy country to get to with a well-developed airport system and international connections.
  - Great rail system.
  - Easy to get around with English.
  - Bike friendly, with many hotels open to bike riding guests.
  - Interesting history and cities.
  - Center of Europe providing opportunities for rides that extend into other countries.

Austria

- o The main ride through Austria covered in this book is my favorite segment of the Danube River.
  - Stretching from Passau on the German Boarder, though Vienna, this is one the easiest and most interesting river segments in Europe.
- o Rides from Salzburg and Innsbruck are also covered.

Cycling Along Europe's Rivers

Hungary

- The central ride covered in this book is the continuation of the Danube River Route. This is quite an interesting segment, but the ride often takes you away from the river, much more so than in Austria or Germany, for example.
- A highlight of this ride is the marvelous city of Budapest.
- Another interesting ride that can serve as an addition to a core Danube ride is around Lake Balaton.

Czech Republic

- The highlight of the river ride in the Czech Republic is Prague.
- It is also possible to start a ride south of Prague on rivers that become the Elbe, at the beautiful city of Cresky Krumlov.
- A nice addition is staying in Cresky Krumlov a couple of days, and doing a day ride south on the river.

Switzerland

- Many interesting routes, but the focus in this book is around Lake Bodensee and the Rhine's descent from the Alps.
- Expensive: I estimate 40 percent more than Germany .
- Excellent bike friendly train system, but expensive.

France

- There are many interesting rivers in France, including the canal network. If you like hills there are also other fantastic opportunities.
- In this book we will look at a great ride from Orleans to the Atlantic Ocean along the Loire River. Castles, Chateaus, great food— what more could you want!
- Also sections from Metz to Trier on the Mosel River, and Strasbourg to Colmar near Rhine.
- France is less bike touring friendly than Germany, including fewer bike accessible trains.

Italy

- As is the case with many countries, there are terrific rides in many parts of Italy, many on roads and involving considerable climbing.
- The rides focused on in this book are in the north. One is the Po River from Milan to Venice, which has many scenic towns, but is not that scenic of a river given the river pollution (at least in 2005 when I rode this route.)
- There are also some rides further north, from Austria, that can get you to Venice. These rides involve hills, but are generally downhill following the Alps to the sea, so the hills can work in your favor!
- The infrastructure, such as trains and boats, are not quite as good in Italy as other places mentioned in this book, but they are acceptable.

Netherlands

- The Netherlands also offers particularly good riding. The Netherlands are known to have more bike riders per capita than any other western country.
- As a point of comparison, there are about 100 million bicycles in the U.S., 32 percent of the population. In the Netherlands, there are about 16.5 million bicycles, amounting to nearly 100 percent of the population. By the way, Germany has 62 million bicycles, amounting to 76 percent of the population.
- The country as a whole is built around bike riding, with great bike trails and signage. People take bikes everywhere and use them extensively for commuting. There is probably no place in Europe you will feel more comfortable riding.
- One of the flattest places you can ride anywhere. In fact, much of the country would be underwater albeit for a levee system.
- This book covers the ride from Amsterdam to Rotterdam along the north coast, and then down the Rhine toward Germany, as well as the ride from Amsterdam to Hamburg.

When to Go and Weather Considerations

I admit I don't like riding in rain or cold, or into a long headwind. If those conditions don't bother you, there is much more flexibility in deciding when and where to ride. But if they are relevant, please consider the following:

- **Seasons**: The Spring tends to have more rain, so we like to ride late Summer and Fall.
- **Summer/Vacations**: Europeans vacation July through about August 20, so we tend to avoid that period. The main reason is we like to ride without hotel reservations and having the flexibility to stop when we find something interesting. However, if you need to ride during the summer months, such as if you are riding with kids, then it is advisable to do more planning on the route, and make hotel reservations at some locations (for example, check to see if a larger town has a conference or event taking place, which can put added pressure on hotels). This is especially important if cost is a factor, since lower cost hotels and special hotels can book up. Another problem with mid-summer riding is that airfares can be higher.
- **When to Head South**: If you are riding in Northern Europe, through mid-August is a good period, since it can get colder later in the summer. During a recent ride north of Hamburg in mid-August it was often in the high 50's and low 60's and rainy! Southern Europe has advantages if riding after August. If you are going in September or October, you might want to ride south of Frankfurt and Dresden.
- **Sweet Spot**: Generally, August 15 through Labor day is a good period for a trip, and September can be great -- although hotels can actually get more crowded again in September.
- **Wind**: Plan your trip so that you are riding with the prevailing wind behind you as much as possible. There are few more unpleasant riding experiences than day after day of stiff headwinds. This information can be researched looking at weather sites. You will never be certain since weather can be unpredictable, but you can use this research for the best guess and your research will usually be right for most of the ride. If you are doing a circular route back

to a starting point, consider using trains to move around so that you can avoid riding into a headwind. Some purist might not like this, preferring to do the entire ride without boarding a train. That is fine, of course, but others might want to go around 180 degrees, then train to a point where another ride can commence with the wind behind or on the side of the planned loop.

- **Weather Charts**: The best thing is to study the average weather charts on places you are looking at going, and see what the temperatures and especially the rain averages predict.

Language Considerations

The rides recommended in this book can all be undertaken without any knowledge of local languages, just English. Don't be intimidated if you don't know German, for example. Most people in Europe speak some English. In Germany the English tends to be very good. But here are a few considerations:

- Learn some key words in the local language. Here are a few suggestions that are good to know just so you can talk a bit, and be polite:
  - Thank you
  - Hello
  - Water
  - Train Station/Airport
  - Hotel
  - How Far?
  - Bike Trail
  - Bicycle
  - A few key food words, such as pork, beef, chicken, fish, for reading menus.
- If you come across a rare situation where the other party does not speak English, find other ways to communicate. Point at something or a book. Use the translation function in your iTouch or phone.
- But don't worry, language will not be a problem.

PART TWO

The Rides

Please note that the following routes sometimes overlap and the same information is contained in multiple routes. I have chosen to try and make each route as self-contained as possible, especially for the Rhine River, which has required some level of redundancy.

Three Main Rivers

This book focuses on rides along three main rivers, various routes that connect these rivers, and a few smaller rivers that connect to these rivers. These rivers are the Rhine: the Danube, and the Elbe. The book also deals with a few additional rivers in France and Italy.

Route Review Rating Guide

One to Five Stars: Five Stars is the Best or the most Challenging

Interesting: The sites, the history, the variety, the beauty are all considered — the more interesting, the more stars.

Navigation: The more stars, the relatively more complicated the routes. All the routes are relatively easy, but this is just to provide distinction among the routes since some are easier than others.

Challenging: Although all the routes are generally flat and easy, some involve longer distances and a few more hills, so the higher the stars, the more challenging — but all the routes in this book are accessible by all.

Rhine River

All-in-all the Rhine River is my favorite touring river in the world. Stretching from the Swiss Alps to the North Sea just past Rotterdam in the Netherlands, the Rhine is over 760 miles long. The good news is there is a bike trail that covers much of that distance, weaving past some of the most scenic, diverse, and historic areas in Europe. These bike trails, or Ragwegs as they are known in Germany, sometimes go right along the banks of the river, or on dikes above the river. On other segments, the bike tour will go inland by as much as a couple of miles. But generally, on these rides you are never far from the grand river.

The Rhine has played an important historic, economic, and military role in Europe. During the Second World War, it was one of the most strategic natural barriers to an invasion of Germany by the Allies. *A Bridge Too Far* and *Bridge at Remagen* are two films that portray this struggle. The Rhine is also a vibrant shipping lane, Europe's most important inland waterway. Modern container ships as well as older bulk cargo ships vie for space on its crowed channels.

I have ridden along the Rhine several times, and never get bored with its diverse, scenic, and interesting sights.

Several interesting rivers also connect to the Rhine, providing enjoyable opportunities to create interesting rides and loops along these smaller rivers and back again to the Rhine. These rivers include the following covered in this book: the Mosel (Moselle), the Neckar, and the Main.

The following are a few routes and combinations I would suggest, but you can also create your own!

Dusseldorf to Wiesbaden/Mainz (Rhine Gorge)

This is a great ride to start your touring, interesting history and sites, short distances, easy logistics:

Interesting: *****

Navigation: *

Challenging: *

Ride Highlights

If you only ride one segment of the Rhine, do this route.

One of the simplest first rides you can do, almost entirely along the River.

Great train and boat infrastructure.

Bike-Friendly Hop on and off River Cruise Ships.

Flexible Route with short and longer distances possible.

Easier than most to rent a bike (in Frankfurt) and do a short trip as part of a longer European trip.

Castles

Dusseldorf

Cologne

Bonn

Remagen (The Bridge Too Far)

Koblenz

Miles and Days

Dusseldorf to Weisbadan: 146 Miles
3-5 Days

Esterbauer Book(s) Needed

Rhein-Radweg (3)

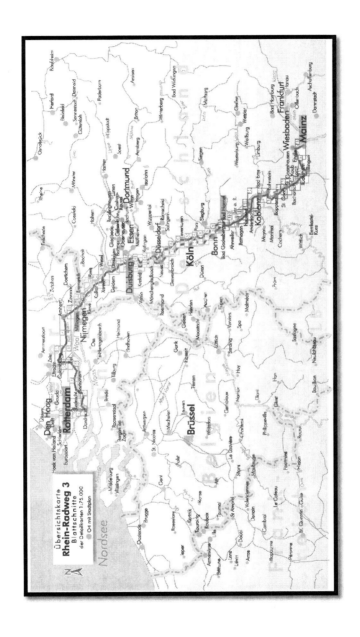

Dusseldorf

Castle above the Rhine

Dusseldorf to Wiesbaden/Mainz (Rhine Gorge)

Bad Breisig

Bike Trail along Rhine

Early Morning on Rhine

Rhine Gorge Cities

Dusseldorf to Wiesbaden/Mainz (Rhine Gorge)

Rhine Gorge Cities

Cycling Along Europe's Rivers

Ride Features

- Fly in and out of Frankfurt Airport.
- Stay at Sheraton Hotel at airport on last night, make prior reservation, can walk across bridge once you clear customs on arrival, and leave bike boxes for duration of trip.
- Train to Dusseldorf.
- Spend the remainder of the day in Dusseldorf, and night, or head out and begin ride.
- Because it is possible to ride this route quickly, or at a slower pace, I will list a few of the more interesting places to visit and also spend the night. This route is easy to customize to whatever pace or distances are comfortable.
- Dusseldorf to Zons, 18 Miles. A nice small town and a potential stop on your first day if want a short day or if you started from Dusseldorf late in the day.
- Zons to Cologne, 16 Miles. Cologne is another great stop for a night, an interesting major city to explore, being Germany's fourth largest city, and home to its famous cathedral.
- Cologne to Bonn, 19 Miles. Bonn is another interesting stop, the former capital of West Germany. It is a pleasant town to spend the night.
- Bonn to Remagen, 15 Miles. An interesting sightseeing stop, the location of a famous bridge over the Rhine that proved one of the most strategic targets late in WW2 as the last bridge left standing across the river. The bridge was captured by the Allies, and was latter a subject of a movie. Not recommended overnight compared to alternatives.
- Remagen to Bad Breisig, 4 Miles. A nice small town, and a good place for a stop to experience a smaller resort river town. Hotels and restaurants along the embankment, many with good views of the river.
    - Recommendation: Hotel Anker along the river is a good buy with simple rooms, and restaurant downstairs.

- o Note. If you would like to ride directly to Cochem up the Mosel, Bad Breisig makes a good stop, with a lunch stop in Koblenz before heading up the Mosel.
- Bad Breisig to Koblenz, 22 Miles.
- Stay night in Koblenz, explore the city, including the wonderful ride over the river to the Ehrenbreitstein Fortress.
    - o Recommendation: The **Hotel Haus Morjan**, good location on the river with balconies. www.Hotel-Morjan.de.
- Note: There are many places to stop along the next stretch, and an extra day can easily be added for shorter rides, more time cruising the river, or riding on the other side of the river, but here is one plan:
- Koblenz to Oberwesel, 30 Miles. Stop at Boppard, and night at Oberwesel.
    - o Recommendation: One of my favorite hotels, **Auf Schonburg** (www.burghotel-schoenburg.de), a castle converted to hotel, overlooking the Rhine, beautiful restaurant, worth the higher price (which includes 4 course dinner) and climb!
    - o Special way to spend near end of a trip.
- Oberwesel to Eltville or Mainz (under 35 Miles). Explore Bingen, Rudesheim, Kaub, and Bacharach along the route.
- Several boats run this route many times a day. This provides an opportunity to ride the boats for an hour for a coffee or lunch break, or gives some riders a chance to do more miles while other riders take a longer break. An attractive stretch to cruise is from St. Gore to Bacharach, which takes you past the famous Lorelei Rock and the narrowest part of the river between Switzerland and the North Sea, and the inspiration for famous music and poems.
    - o Here are some boat lines:
        - www.k-d.com.
        - www.loreley-linie.de.
        - www.bingen-ruedesheimer.de.
        - www.rnf-schifffahrt.de.
- Ride back to Frankfurt Airport and directly to hotel.

- From Eltville, stay on Rhine River until reach Main River, then head north toward Frankfurt.
- From Mainz cross Rhine at north side of city heading to Kastel, then south on Rhine and turn onto Main River on north bank. Head toward Frankfurt.

- Cross Main to south bank near Eddersheim or just before Sindlingen.
- Head toward Kelsterbach.
- Get on the Kelsterbach Sud Road toward the Airport.
- About 17 miles from Main/Rhine intersection to the Airport. About 3 miles from Main River to hotels at Airport, with bike lanes available almost entire way. Make sure you take the South Kelsterbach road to avoid traffic.

Mosel River

A good addition to the Dusseldorf to Wiesbaden ride, providing flexibility to add a day or more, and variety to the route:

Interesting: ***

Navigation: *

Challenging: *

Ride Highlights

Great Ride: Beautiful Mosel Valley, covered with numerous vineyards on almost every slope.

A chance to sample many German white wines -- Riesling Grand tour.

Koblenz

Eltz Castle

Cochem

Zell

Traban-Trarbach

Bernkastel-Kues

Trier

Luxembourg and Saar River day ride options

Thionville

Metz

Smaller and quieter than the Rhine River, providing a nice contrast.

Miles and Days

180 Miles

6 to 9 Days, depending on how much of the river you would like to ride, your pace, and your schedule.

Esterbauer Book(s) Needed

Moselle River Trail — In English

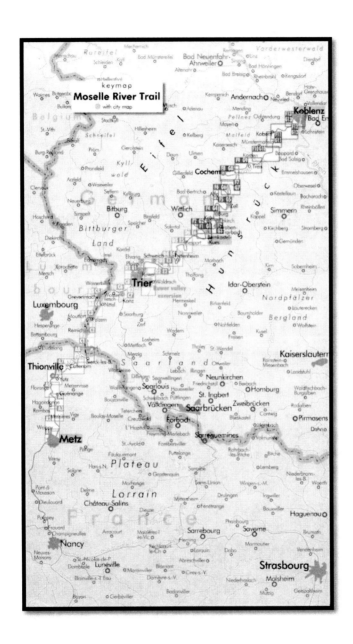

Cycling Along Europe's Rivers

Alt Thorschenke Hotel Cochem

Along the Mosel

Mosel River

Bike Trail along the Mosel

Vineyards along the Mosel River

Cycling Along Europe's Rivers

Along The Mosel

Castle above the Moselle

Mosel River

Boat from Cochem to Koblenz

Cycling Along Europe's Rivers

Ride Features

- Fly into and out of Frankfurt Airport.
- Reserve airport Sheraton or Hilton hotel, or other nearby hotel for last night of trip, and leave bike boxes at reserved hotel.
- **Metz Start:** If starting at Metz, take train to Metz (Airport (9:59 AM)-Mainz-Karlsruhe-Strasbourg). Consider night in interesting city of Strasbourg, or spend few hours looking around before 1.5 hour train ride to Metz. Total train rides about 6 hours -- Airport to Metz. Going to Metz does add travel time, but interesting city and provides added French/Alsace experience (and food!).
  - Recommendation: **Hotel de la Cathedral**, well-located, friendly, nice dinner, and reasonable priced. www.hotelcathedral-metz.fr.
- Metz to Perl. 30 Miles.
  - Option: Quick train to Thionville, then ride to Trier if in hurry (56 miles).
- Perl to Trier. 32 Miles. Cross the river and stop in the pretty town of Remich to experience a break in Luxembourg. Map "C" Right Bank.
- **Trier Start**: If starting in Trier, train (Frankfurt Airport to Trier, changing in Koblenz, total under 3 hours). Enjoy the Roman ruins, old town, and museums.
  - Recommendation: Stay at the **Hotel Villa Hugel** in Trier. This 1914 house with 36 rooms, good views, pool, and great breakfast (10 min. walk from city center). www.hotel-villa-huegel.de/en.
  - Options: Consider a few nights in Trier, leaving bags at hotel for interesting day rides to: (1) Luxembourg City, and (2) down the Saar River to Saarburg, Mettlach and the beautiful Saarchleife. (Bikeline "Velo Route SaarLor Lux" Book useful.)
- Trier to Bernkastel-Kues (37 miles) or to Traban/Trarbach (50 miles). Both make great overnights. BK a bit more interesting (wine museum), TT very pleasant and cycle/toy museums. From Trier head out on south side of Mosel along river, a bit confusing

until Ruwer, so pay attention, from then to BK stay on the Map "E" side of the Mosel. BK to TT stay on Map "G" side of the Mosel.

- o Recommendation: **Hotel Bellevue** in TT, great view/ good breakfast. Higher priced but nice stay. Splurge for room with balcony. www.bellevue-hotel.de.
- o Consider a boat ride for part of the trip between KK and Koblenz, they run on regular basis.
  - www.moselfahrplan.de
  - www.mosel-schiffstouristik.de.
- o Great bike repair shop in BK, Schanzstrabe 22.
- BK or TT to beautiful medieval city of Cochem (50 or 37 miles).BK to TT, stay on Map "G" side of Mosel, TT to Cochem, stay on Map "F" side of Mosel, except for crossing to attractive city of Zell for lunch/break.
  - o Recommendation: Cochem stay at the historic **Alte Thorschenke hotel,** with original buildings dating to 1332. www.castle-thorschenke.com. Book ahead.
- Cochem to Koblenz (30 miles), with stop in Moselkern to ride up to Eltz Castle (or take taxi up). Consider night in Moselkern/ Munstermaifeld if time given detour/hills. Ride on Plan "F" maps on NW side of river, cross into Koblenz at Schumacher Brucke.
- Explore Koblenz, including the spectacular ride to the Ehrenbreitstein Fortress.
  - o Recommendation: The **Hotel Haus Morjan**, good location on the river with balconies.www.Hotel-Morjan.de.
- Train back to Frankfurt Airport, or to Mainz and ride 22 miles from Mainz train station to Frankfurt Airport and hotels: Cross Rhine north Mainz heading to Kastel, south on Rhine and turn onto Main River on north bank, toward Frankfurt, cross Main to south bank near Eddersheim or before Sindlingen, head to Kelsterbach Sud Road and then to Airport and your hotel.
- o Option: Ride south on Rhine, stopping at Boppard, and night at Oberwesel at one of my favorite hotels, **Auf Schonburg** (www.burghotel-schoenburg.de), a castle overlooking the Rhine, worth the higher price (inc. 4 course dinner) and climb! Great way to end a trip. Then ride to Mainz (37 miles) or Frankfurt Airport (54 Miles.) Consider train or boats part of the way.

Mosel and Rhine Gorge

One of my favorite routes, easy navigation and logistics, and plenty to see, with route distances very flexible:

Interesting: *****

Navigation: *

Challenging: *

Ride Highlights

One of my favorite routes: A great combination of a large river and a smaller river.

Easy access to Frankfurt Airport and roundtrip flights.

Great train and boat infrastructure.

Bike-Friendly Hop on and off River Cruise Ships.

Flexible Route with short and longer distances possible.

Castles

Dusseldorf

Cologne

Bonn

Remagen (The Bridge Too Far)

Koblenz

Beautiful Mosel Valley, covered with numerous vineyards on almost every slope.

A chance to sample many German white wines, and a wine tour

Cochem, Traben-Trarbach, Bernkastel-Kues, Trier, Metz

Mosel and Rhine Gorge

Miles and Days

115 on Mosel, 150 Miles on Rhine
8-12 Days

Esterbauer Book(s) Needed

Rhine-Radweg (3)
Mosel River Trail (English)

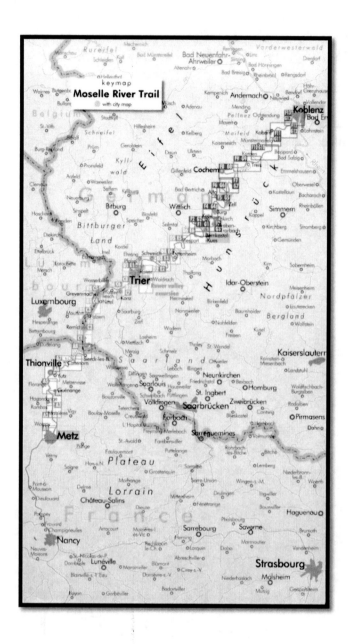

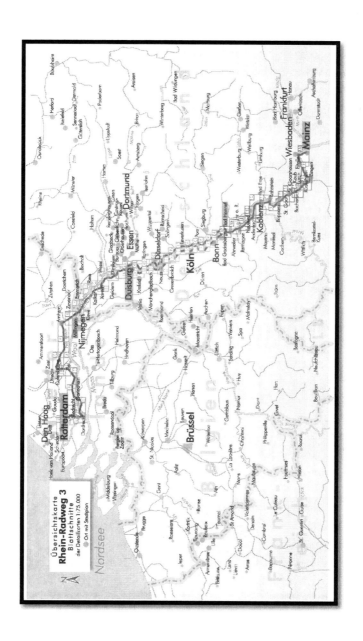

Cycling Along Europe's Rivers

Ride Features

- Fly in and out of Frankfurt.
- Reserve airport Sheraton or Hilton hotel, or other nearby hotel for last night of trip, and leave bike boxes at reserved hotel.
- Potential to rent a bike in Frankfurt, if so, take train to airport.
- Train to Dusseldorf (reserve ahead for bikes if can, about 3 hour trip, leaving about 10 AM, for example).
- Stay night in Dusseldorf or set off on ride.
- This route is easy to customize to whatever pace or distances are comfortable.
- Dusseldorf to Zons, 18 Miles. A nice small town and a potential stop on your first day if want a short day or started from Dusseldorf late in the day.
- Zons to Cologne, 16 Miles. Cologne is another great stop for a night, an interesting city to explore, being Germany's fourth largest city, and home to its famous cathedral.
- Cologne to Bonn, 19 Miles. Bonn is another interesting stop, the former capital of West Germany. Fine night stop.
- Bonn to Remagen, 15 Miles. An interesting sightseeing location, the site of a famous bridge over the Rhine that proved one of the most strategic targets late in WW2 as the last bridge left standing across the river. The bridge was captured by the Allies, and was latter subject of a movie.
- Remagen to Bad Breisig, 4 Miles. A good overnight -- experience a smaller resort river town. Hotels and restaurants along the embankment, many with good views of the river.
    - Recommendation: Hotel Anker along the river is a good buy with simple rooms, and restaurant downstairs.
- Bad Breisig to Koblenz, 22 Miles. Take Train from Koblenz to Trier. Train ride about 21E and 90 to 120 minutes.
- Trier. Enjoy the Roman ruins, old town, and museums.
    - Recommendation: Stay at the **Hotel Villa Hugel** in Trier. This 1914 house with 36 rooms, good views, pool, and great breakfast (10 min. walk to city center). www.hotel-villa-huegel.de/en.

Mosel and Rhine Gorge

- o Options: Consider a few nights in Trier, leaving bags at hotel for interesting day rides to: (1) Luxembourg City, and (2) down the Saar River to Saarburg, Mettlach and the beautiful Saarchleife. (Bikeline "Velo Route SaarLor Lux" Book useful.)
- Trier to Bernkastel-Kues (37 miles) or to Traban/Trarbach (50 miles). Both make great overnights. BK a bit more interesting (Wine Museum), TT very pleasant and Cycle/Toy Museums. From Trier head out on south side of Mosel along river, a bit confusing until Ruwer, so pay attention, from then to BK stay on the Map "E" side of the Mosel. BK to TT stay on Map "G" side of the Mosel.
  - o Recommendation: **Hotel Bellevue** in TT, great view/ good breakfast. Higher priced but nice stay. Splurge for room with balcony. www.bellevue-hotel.de.
  - o Consider a boat ride for part of the trip between KK and Koblenz, they run on regular basis.
    - www.moselfahrplan.de
    - www.mosel-schiffstouristik.de.
  - o Great bike repair shop in BK, "Fun Bike Team", Schanzstrabe 22, 06531-94024.
- BK or TT to beautiful medieval city of Cochem (50 or 37 miles). BK to TT, stay on Map "G" side of Mosel, TT to Cochem, stay on Map "F" side of Mosel, except for crossing to attractive city of Zell for lunch/break.
  - o Recommendation: Cochem stay at the historic **Alte Thorschenke hotel,** with original buildings dating to 1332. www.castle-thorschenke.com. Book ahead.
- Cochem to Koblenz (30 miles), with stop in Moselkern to ride up to Eltz Castle (or take taxi up). Consider night in Moselkern/ Munstermaifeld if time given detour/hills. Ride on Plan "F" maps on NW side of river, cross into Koblenz at Schumacher Brucke. Moselkern to Koblenz, ok ride, but one of my least favorite Mosel stretches, good boat ride section.
- Explore Koblenz, including the spectacular ride over river to the Ehrenbreitstein Fortress.

- o Recommendation: The **Hotel Haus Morjan**, good location on the river with balconies. www.Hotel-Morjan.de.
- Koblenz to Oberwesel, 32 Miles. Stop at Boppard, and night at Oberwesel.
  - o Recommendation: One of my favorite hotels, **Auf Schonburg** (www.burghotel-schoenburg.de), a castle overlooking the Rhine, beautiful restaurant (4 course dinner included), worth the higher price (120-160E pp per night) and climb! Special way to end a trip.
- Oberwesel to Eltville or Mainz (under 35 Miles). Explore Bingen, Rudesheim, Kaub, and Bacharach along the route.
- Several boats run this route many times a day. This provides an opportunity to ride the boats for an hour for a coffee or lunch break, or gives some riders a chance to do more miles while other riders take a longer break. An attractive stretch to cruise is from St. Gore to Bacharach, which takes you past the famous Lorelei Rock and the narrowest part of the river between Switzerland and the North Sea, and the inspiration for famous music and poems.
  - o Here are some boat lines:
    - www.k-d.com.
    - www.loreley-linie.de.
    - www.bingen-ruedesheimer.de.
    - www.rnf-schifffahrt.de.
- Ride back to Frankfurt Airport and directly to hotel.
- From Eltville, stay on Rhine River until reach Main River, then head north. From Mainz cross Rhine at north side of city heading to Kastel, then south on Rhine and turn onto Main River on north bank. Head toward Frankfurt.
- Cross Main to south bank near Eddersheim or just before Sindlingen, head to Kelsterbach, get on the Kelsterbach Sud Road toward the Airport and hotels. About 17 miles from Main/Rhine intersection to the Airport. About 3 miles from river to hotels at Airport, with bike lanes available almost entire way. Make sure you take the South Kelsterbach road to avoid traffic.

Main River

A good addition to the Rhine and quite an easy route, although there can be some longer stretches unless you stop in smaller towns, and hilly in the beginning (away from Frankfurt), although this can be skipped by starting closer to Frankfurt:

Interesting: ***

Navigation: **

Challenging: **

Ride Highlights

Potential to do Roundtrip from Frankfurt using a rented bike.

Good, easy trail, especially from Hassfurt (HaBfurt) to Mainz.

Good rail infrastructure, and boats in places.

Bayreuth

Bamberg

Wurzburg

Aschaffenburg

Frankfurt

Mixture of small and larger towns.

Good add-on to the Rhine or other rivers.

Miles and Days

310 Miles
Up to 8 Days

Esterbauer Book(s) Needed

Main-Radweg

Main River

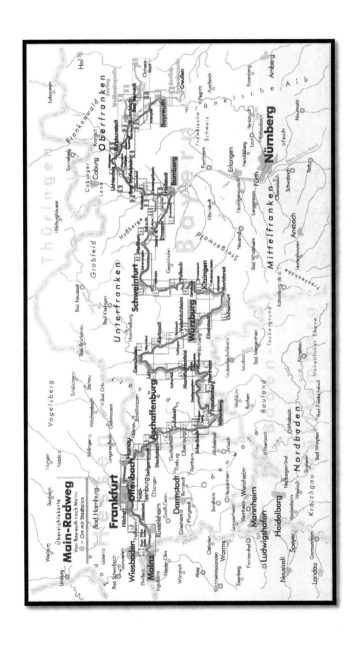

Wurzburg

Along the Trail

Main River

Castle and Town along the Main

Towns along ride from Wurzburg to Aschaffenburg

Towns along ride from Wurzburg to Aschaffenburg

Aschaffenburg Castle

Main River

Entering Frankfurt

Along the Main in Frankfurt

Cycling Along Europe's Rivers

Ride Features

- Fly in and out of Frankfurt.
- Reserve the Sheraton or other hotel near the airport for your last night and take your bike boxes to the hotel after clearing customs upon arrival.
- Potential to rent a bike in Frankfurt, if so, take train to city.
- Take train to Bayreuth.
- Spend night in Bayreuth, or head out.
- Bayreuth to Kulmbach. This ride is along a modest sized road, about 16 miles. If you arrive in Bayreuth and want to ride some the first day, Kulmbach makes a good overnight stop.
  - Option: There are also a couple of optional excursions during this part of the ride.
- Kulmbach to Lichtenfels, 21 miles, the small Main river starts to appear.
- Lichtenfels to Bamberg, 29 miles. Bamberg makes a good overnight stop. If you can get to Kulbach the first day, it is a nice 50 mile ride to Bamberg, or break the trip in Lichtenfels.
- Bamberg to Hassfurt, 23 miles.
- Hassfurt to Schweinfurt, 15 miles. The ride now starts to stay close to the river, and the river has transformed from a stream to a small river. Schweinfurt makes a good stop, about 38 miles from Bamberg.
- Schwenfurt to Volkach, 18 miles.
- Volkach to Kitzengen, 18 miles. There is a choice of sides of the river for this section, and a chance to ferry across at Mainstockheim. Another overnight possible at Kitzengen at 36 miles.
- Kitzengen to Ochsenfurt, 11 miles. I recommend the southern side of river until Ochensfurt, then cross to the northern side of the river.
- Ochsenfurt to Wurzburg, 13 miles.
  - Recommendation:
    - Wurzburg is a recommended stop, even if you get in early, plenty to see and do.

Main River

- Consider the Hotel Wurzburger Hof.
- Wurzburg to Karlstadt, 17 miles. The ride from here to Frankfurt becomes an increasingly interesting river ride, as the Main River increases in size. The stretch to Karlstadt is especially attractive and Karlstadt is a charming small town for a break.
- Karlstadt to Lohr, 18 miles. On this ride you pass through Gemunden am Main, which also makes a good break or an overnight if not riding to Lohr or beyond.
- Lohr to Marktheidenfeld, 12 miles. Another nice stop at Marktheidenfeld.
- Marktheidenfeld to Wertheim, 14 miles.
  - Recommendation:
    - Wertheim makes a very good overnight stop. I rode from Wurzburg to Wertheim last trip, but it was a long ride and would recommend a break if have the time.
    - Consider the Hotel Kette. Simple rooms, nice setting and reasonable price.www.tauberhotel-kette.de.
- Wetheim to Miltenberg, 21 miles. Miltenberg makes another good overnight spot.
- Miltenberg to Klingenberg, 9 miles. Good snack break spot, including restaurant castle on the hill above the river.
- Klingenberg to Aschaffenburg, 16 miles. Aschaffenburg makes good overnight from Wetheim, 46 miles. Its famous Johannisburg Palace and Gardens were built from 1605-1614.
  - Recommendation: Try the cafe restaurant in front of Palace facing the river.
- Aschaffenburg to Seligenstadt, 11 miles.
- Seligenstadt to Offenbach am Main, 18 miles. Steinheim am Main and Kesselstadt both worth a look.
- Now you are on the outskirts of Frankfurt. Only another 4 miles to Frankfurt.
  - Options:
    - Riders can stop for the night in Frankfurt, or continue directly to airport (Flughafen).
    - To Airport, head west on Main River toward Mainz and the Rhine River, on south side of the river, turn off

at Kelsterbach, take Kelsterbach Sud road to Airport and hotels (about 3 miles from Main River). Bike path most of the way.

Neckar River

A good addition to the Rhine, especially the first half from the Rhine that includes Heidelberg, but if you want to do entire route, start near Villingen so you can ride downhill back toward the Rhine:

Interesting: ***

Navigation: **

Challenging: ***

Ride Highlights

Roundtrip flights to Frankfurt.

Good train infrastructure, but not as good as Rhine.

Opportunity to do Roundtrip from Frankfurt and rent a bike.

A quite river that takes you off the Rhine and visit Heidelberg.

Variety of lengths and directions possible.

Ride the entire length from Villingen back to the Rhine, or start at Tubingen or even Stuttgart for more of a "river" ride, flat ride.

Heidelberg, one of the prettiest smaller cities in Europe.

Stuttgart and the car museums.

The small scenic river, especially from Stuttgart to Heidelberg.

Tubingen

Miles and Days

240 Miles
Up to 6 Days.

Esterbauer Book(s) Needed

Neckar-Radweg

Neckar River

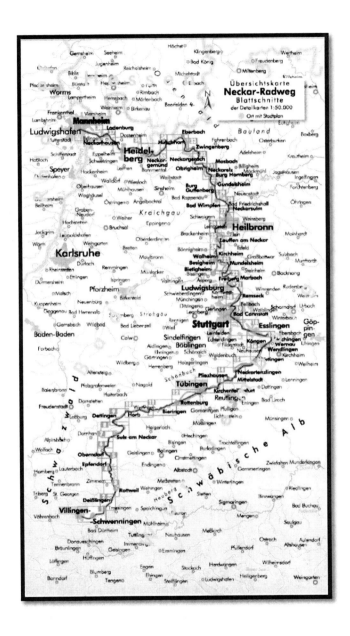

Heidelberg

Heidelberg

Neckar River

Ride along the Neckar

Ride along the Neckar

View from Bad Wimpfen

Vineyards' along the Trail

Neckar River

Vineyards' along the Trail

Riding the Trail

Cycling Along Europe's Rivers

Ride Features

- Fly in and out of Frankfurt.
- Reserve the Sheraton or other hotel near the airport for your last night and take your bike boxes to hotel after clearing customs upon arrival.
- Potential to rent a bike in Frankfurt, if so, take train to city.
- If you want to ride full route, take train to Villengen.
- The first part of this route has some hills, but beyond several climbs, most of the ride is downhill.
- Villengen to Schwenningen, 5.5 miles. The first part of this ride you won't really notice a river, just a small stream from time-to-time.
- Schwenningen to Rottweil, 12 miles. The ride is often on bike trail along small roads. Rottweil is a potential stop for the night.
- Rottweil to Oberndorf am Neckar, 12 miles. At this point a more developed bike route begins.
- Oberndorf to Sulz am Neckar, 7 miles. There are a few small hills on this segment, also some unpaved segments. Sulz is a picturesque town.
- Sulz to Horb am Neckar, 11 miles. Horb makes a good night stop.
- Horb to Rottenburg am Neckar, 15 miles. Next segment has a few hills and unpaved segments. Rottenburg is also town for a potential stop.
- Rottenburg to Tubingen, 8 miles. Turbingen is one of the more interesting stops of the ride thus far and a recommended stop. Tubingen might also be a city to start your ride if you would like to make it shorter, or involving less hills and unpaved trails.
- Tubingen to Nurtingen, 18 miles. A potential stop.
- Nurtingen to Stuttgart 21 miles. Stuttgart makes an interesting stop, especially for car enthusiasts. See the Mercedes-Benz Museum.
- Stuttgart to Ludwigsburg, 13 miles. From this point on the Neckar starts to look more like a small river and becomes more scenic. Going into Ludwigsburg is uphill, an interesting town, but you

need to be willing to climb. Note that the train station is far from the river and uphill in this town.

- Ludwigsburg to Besigheim, 16 miles. A stop in Besigheim or Bietigheim possible.
- Besigheim to Helibronn, 15 miles. Helibronn is a good stop. I would recommend the stop at Heilbronn or Bad Wimpfen.
- Heilbronn to Bad Wimpfen, 8 miles.
  - o Recommendation: The Hotel am Rosengarten in Bad Wimpfen worked well. It also has a large outdoor spa attached next door, for a pleasant heated outdoor or indoor swim.
- Bad WimpfentoNeckargerach19 miles. The river becomes even more scenic.
  - o Recommendation: Near Neckarwestheim, the Schloshotel Liebenstein is quite nice, out of our typical price target, but consider a coffee and strudel on its beautiful roof terrace — you will deserve it after the climb up!www.schlosshotel-liebenstein.com.
- Neckargerach to Hirschhorn, 13 miles. At Hirschhorn the Burg Hirschhorn.
- Hirschhorn to Heidelberg, 15.5 miles.
  - o Recommendation:
    - Heidelberg is one of the special towns in Europe. It was never destroyed during WW2, it has retained its historic, albeit touristy, charm.
    - A definite stop for one or two nights. Consider the Hotel Hollander Hof, centrally located. More expensive than typical hotels we tend to stay at, but Heidelberg, being a tourist center, is a bit more expensive. www.hollaender-hof.de
    - Consider a boat ride from Heidelberg up the Neckar or to Mannheim at certain times. Boats also sometimes head up the Rhine toward St. Goar, Loreley, Eltville, and Rudesheim. www.rnf-schifffahrt.de.
- Heidelberg to Mannheim, 15 miles.

Cycling Along Europe's Rivers

- o Train back to Frankfurt Airport, or ride the Rhine river north to the Main River, then up the Main River to the Airport.
- o Options:
  - Train back to Frankfurt Airport
  - Ride north on the Rhine to the Airport.
  - Train to Mainz, explore Mainz (overnight if time) and then ride to the Airport.
  - Riding to Airport, head on Main River toward Frankfurt on the north side of the Main, cross the Main just before Sindlingen, head toward Kelsterbach, take Kelsterbach Sud road to Airport and hotels (about 3 miles from River). Bike path most of the way.

Four Rivers Grand Tour: Rhine, Mosel, Neckar, Main

One of my favorite routes on the Rhine, plenty of diversity and interesting sites. Slightly more complicated since moving from river to river, but very manageable and worth it if you have the time:

Interesting: *****

Navigation: ***

Challenging: **

Ride Highlights

Roundtrip From Frankfurt

A really great ride that provides diversity and flexibility to craft a ride from 9 days to well over two weeks.

Easy access from Frankfurt airport, in and out of the same airport.

A grand tour of the middle Rhine and other connecting rivers.

A great combination of a large river and smaller rivers.

Good train and boat infrastructure.

Bike-Friendly Hop on and off River Cruise Ships.

Flexible Route with short and longer distances possible.

Easier than most to rent a bike (in Frankfurt) and do a short trip as part of a longer European trip.

Castles, Dusseldorf, Cologne, Bonn, Koblenz, Heidelberg, Wurzburg

Beautiful Mosel Valley, covered with numerous vineyards on almost every slope.

A chance to sample many German white wines.

Historic towns, with Cochem being a highlight.

And More!

Cycling Along Europe's Rivers

Miles and Days

9 to 14 Plus Days
Up to 880 Miles
My last ride using this route was 525 Miles over 11 Days.

Esterbauer Book(s) Needed

Rhine-Radweg (Volume 2)
Rhine-Radweg (Volume 3)
Main-Radweg
Mosel River Trail (English)
Neckar-Radweg

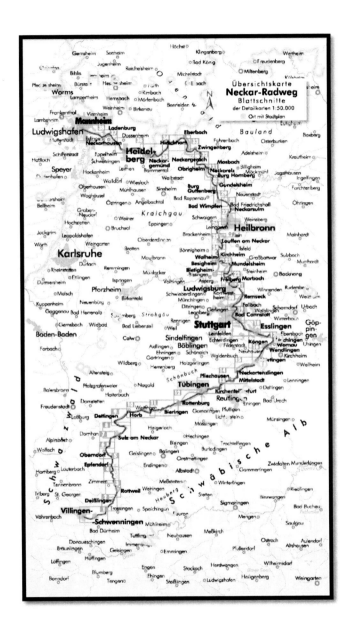

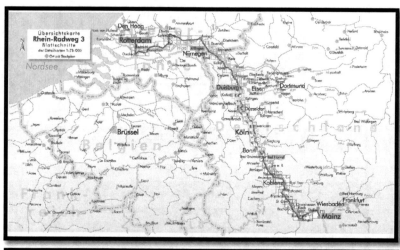

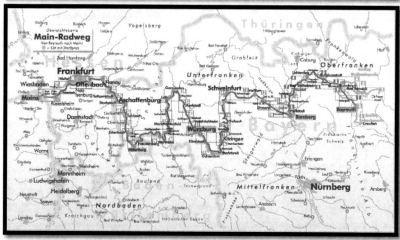

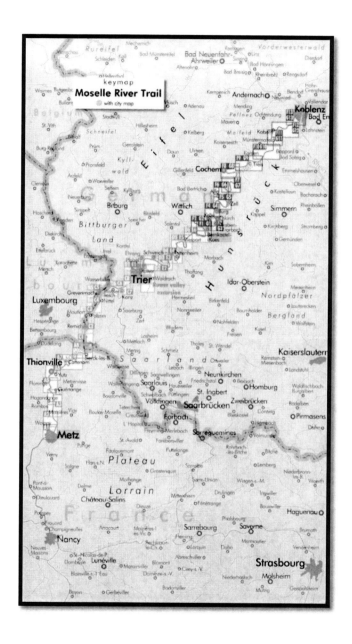

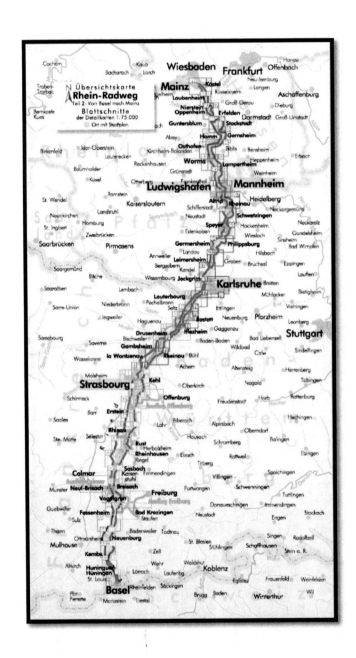

Along the Rhine

Rhine Trail

Rhine Shipping

Four Rivers Grand Tour: Rhine Gorge, Mosel, Neckar, Main

Ride Features

- Fly in and out of Frankfurt.
- Reserve the Sheraton or other hotel near the airport for your last night and take your bike boxes to hotel after clearing customs upon arrival.
- Potential to rent a bike in Frankfurt, if so, take train to city to rental location you have identified.
- Train to Dusseldorf.
- Stay night in Dusseldorf or set off on ride.
- Because it is possible to ride this route quickly, or at a slower pace, I will list a few of the more interesting places to visit and also spend the night. This route is easy to customize to whatever pace or distances are comfortable.
- Dusseldorf to Zons, 18 Miles. A nice small town and a potential stop on your first day if want a short day or started from Dusseldorf late in the day.
- Zons to Cologne, 16 Miles. Cologne is another great stop for a night, an interesting city to explore, being Germany's fourth largest city, and home to its famous cathedral.
- Cologne to Bonn, 19 Miles. Bonn is another interesting stop, the former capital of West Germany. It is a pleasant town to spend the night.
- Bonn to Remagen, 15 Miles. An interesting sightseeing stop, the site of a famous bridge over the Rhine that proved one of the most strategic targets late in WW2 as the last bridge left standing across the river. The bridge was captured by the Allies, and was latter subject of a movie. Not recommended overnight given other options.
- Remagen to Bad Breisig, 4 Miles. A nice small town, and a good place for a stop to experience a smaller resort river town. Hotels and restaurants along the embankment, many with good views of the river.
  - Recommendation: Hotel Anker along the river is a good buy with simple rooms, and restaurant downstairs.

- o Note. If you would like to ride directly to Cochem up the Mosel, Bad Breisig makes a good stop, with a lunch stop in Koblenz before heading up the Mosel.
- Bad Breisig to Koblenz, 22 Miles. Another very good overnight stop, much to see in the city, good ride over the river to Ehrenbreitstein Fortress.
    - o Recommendation: The Hotel Haus Morjan, well-located, rooms on the river with balconies. A bit nicer than our standard hotels, but three stars. Contact couple days ahead. www.Hotel-Morjan.de.
    - o Note. Koblenz is the turn-off for a ride up the Mosel River.
- Ride to the medieval city Cochem, about 30 miles, potential stop at Eltz Castle.
    - o Recommendation: Stay at the historic Alte Thorschenke hotel, with original buildings dating to 1332. www.castle-thorschenke.com.Consider booking ahead.
- Options:
    - o It is possible to take a boat back to Koblenz certain times of the year or ride back on Koblenz (or take the train back).
    - o Tour can continue along the Mosel as per the Mosel route in this book (to Trier), and train back to Koblenz.
    - o Another good option is spending an extra night in Cochem and do a day ride to Traben/Trarbach, 34 miles, and take train/boat back to Cochem.
- Continue ride from Koblenz.
- Koblenz to Wiesbaden, 54 Miles. This stretch provides many options. It can be completed in a day, especially if you use the many boats that cruise this area for part of the ride, such as 10-20 miles during a lunch break onboard. On the other hand, this section can take 3 days, taking ones time at the many charming towns that come one after another along this section of the river. There is probably no nicer section of small attractive towns along the entire Rhine. My advice is to take at least two days if you can, and enjoy.
- Here are some of the nicer towns along this stretch: Lahnstein, Braubach, Boppard, St. Goar, Oberwesel, Kaub, Bacharach, Lorch,

Rudesheim, Bingen, Eltville. On the last stretch from Rudesheim stay on the north bank of the river.

- o Recommendation: Night at Oberwesel at one of my favorite hotels, **Auf Schonburg** (www.burghotel-schoenburg.de), a castle overlooking the Rhine, worth the higher price (inc. 4 course dinner) and climb!

- Several boats run this route many times a day. This provides an opportunity to ride the boats for an hour for a coffee or lunch break, or gives some riders a chance to do more miles while other riders take a longer break. A nice stretch to cruise is from St. Gore to Bacharach, which takes you past the famous Lorelei Rock and the narrowest part of the river between Switzerland and the North Sea, and the inspiration for famous music and poems.

  - o Here are some boat lines:
    - www.k-d.com.
    - www.loreley-linie.de.
    - www.bingen-ruedesheimer.de.
    - www.rnf-schifffahrt.de.

- Recommendation:
  - o Consider staying in Walluf near just west of Wiesbadan (Zum Weissen Mohren Hotel).www.zum-weissen-mohren.de.A good restaurant in town is Zum Treppchen.

- Weisbadan to Mainz, 4 Miles.

- Ride from Mainz to Mannheim, with a potential stop in Worms. Total distance 44-60 miles.
  - o Option: Train from Wiesbaden or Mainz to Mannheim or all the way to Heidelberg. Train from Mainz changes in Ludwigshafen, and takes about 90 minutes from Mainz to Heidelberg.
  - o Worms make a good stop, many interesting sites is this mid-size city.

- Start up the Neckar River, Mannheim to Heidelberg 15 miles.

- Heidelberg is one of the special towns in Europe.
  - o Recommendation:

- Heidelberg is one of the special towns in Europe. It was never destroyed during WW2, it has retained its historic, albeit touristy, charm.
- A definite stop for one or two nights. Consider the Hotel Hollander Hof, centrally located. More expensive, but Heidelberg, being a tourist center, is more expensive. www.hollaender-hof.de
- Consider a boat ride from Heidelberg up the Neckar or to Mannheim at certain times. Boats also sometimes head up the Rhine toward St. Goar, Loreley, Eltville, and Rudesheim. www.rnf-schifffahrt.de.

- Heidelberg to Heilbronn, about 60 miles, or stop at Bad Wimpfen about 49 miles, nice stop.
  - Recommendation: The Hotel am Rosengarten in Bad Wimpfen worked well. It also has a large outdoor spa attached next door.
  - Recommendation: The Schloshotel Liebenstein is quite nice, out of our price target, but consider a coffee and strudel on its beautiful roof terrace — you will deserve it after the climb up!www.schlosshotel-liebenstein.com. Near Neckarwestheim.
  - Option
    - Continue along the Neckar as provided in the Neckar route in this book.
    - Train from Heilbronn to Main River, best stop Wurzburg.
    - Ride from Wurzburg to Frankfurt, as outlined below, or ride further up the Main River.
- Stay in Wurzburg.
  - Recommendation:
    - Wurzburg is a recommended stop, even if you get in early, plenty to see and do.
    - Consider the Hotel Wurzburger Hof.
- Wurzburg to Karlstadt, 17 miles. The ride from here to Frankfurt becomes an increasingly interesting river ride, as the Main River increases size. This stretch to Karlstadt is nice and Karlstadt is a charming small town for a break.

Four Rivers Grand Tour: Rhine Gorge, Mosel, Neckar, Main

- Karlsadt to Lohr, 18 miles. On this ride you pass through Gemunden am Main, which also makes a good break or an overnight if not riding to Lohr or beyond.
- Lohr to Marktheidenfeld, 12 miles. Another nice stop at Maarktheidenfeld.
- Marktheidenfeld to Wertheim, 14 miles. Wertheim makes a very good overnight stop. I rode from Wurzburg to Wertheim last trip, but it was a long ride and would recommend a break if have the time.
- Wetheim to Miltenberg, 21 miles. Miltenberg makes another good overnight spot.
- Miltenberg to Klingenberg, 9 miles. Good snack break spot, including restaurant castle on the hill above the river.
- Klingenberg to Aschaffenburg, 16 miles. Aschaffenburg makes good overnight from Wetheim, 46 miles.
  - Recommendation: Visit the Schloss Johannisburg, and have a snack or meal at the restaurant in front of the Palace facing the river.
- Aschaffenburg to Seligenstadt, 11 miles.
- Seligenstadt to Offenbach am Main, 18 miles. Steinheim am Main and Kesselstadt both worth a look.
- Now you are on the outskirts of Frankfurt. Only another 4 miles to Frankfurt.
  - Options:
    - Riders can stop for the night in Frankfurt, or continue directly to airport (Flughafen).
    - To Airport, head west on Main River toward Mainz and the Rhine River, on south side of the Main River, turn off at Kelsterbach, take Kelsterbach Sud road to Airport and hotels (about 3 miles from Main River). Bike path most of the way.

Amsterdam to Rotterdam, Rhine to Frankfurt

A good mixture of sites and interesting cities, a variety of cultures, a bit more complicated than most other rides especially the first sections, but quite manageable.

Interesting: *****

Navigation: ***

Challenging: **

Ride Highlights

Flat well-marked route through bike friendly Holland.

Chance to ride in Holland and Germany.

Reasonably good rail system (not as good as core of Rhine).

Bike-Friendly Hop On and Off River Cruise Ships for some segments.

Windmills and Cheese.

Amsterdam, Haarlan, Leiden, The Hague, Rotterdam (near the mouth of the Rhine), Utrecht

Arnhem — battleground and museums, extraordinary Kroller-Muller Museum.

Castles

Rhine Gorge, Dusseldorf, Cologne, Bonn, Remagen (The Bridge Too Far), Koblenz

---

Amsterdam to Rotterdam, Rhine to Frankfurt

Miles and Days

65 Miles from Amsterdam to Rotterdam, along North Sea, but there are also shorter more direct routes.
370 Miles from Rotterdam to Mainz.

Esterbauer Book(s) Needed

Rhein-Radweg (3)
Nordseekusten-Radweg

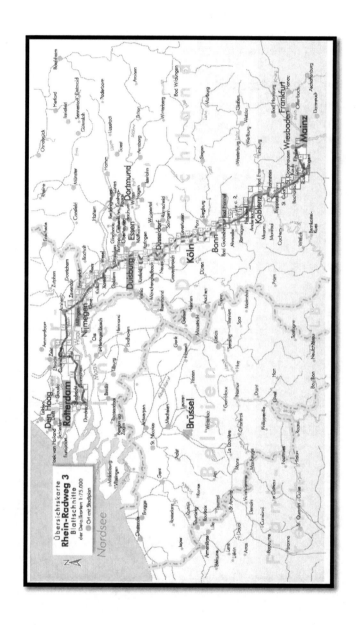

Amsterdam to Rotterdam, Rhine to Frankfurt

Dunes Along North Sea

North Sea Beach

Cycling Along Europe's Rivers

Mouth of the Rhine

Rotterdam

Amsterdam to Rotterdam, Rhine to Frankfurt

Windmills in Holland

Cheese in Gouda

House in Holland along Trail

Kroller-Muller Museum

Amsterdam to Rotterdam, Rhine to Frankfurt

Arnhem Cemetery

Near Tolkamer at the German Boarder

Along the Rhine with Castle

Amsterdam to Rotterdam, Rhine to Frankfurt

Ride Features

- Fly into Amsterdam. This is a point-to-point ride, so you need to mail your bike box to your destination in Frankfurt, for example the Sheraton hotel at the airport. You can also use disposable boxes furnished by airline, and it is usually possible to get a new box at Frankfurt airport.
- Ride right out of the Amsterdam Airport in this country with more bikes per capita than the United States, and many well-marked bike trails.
- Options:
  - Head into Amsterdam and enjoy the city.
  - Start your ride and head toward Haarlen.
- Ride to Haarlen from Airport or Amsterdam, about 15 miles.
- Haarlen to Leiden, 18 miles by riding from Haarlem west to the North Sea, then follow the route until Katwijkaan Zee, then head south-east to Leiden. Most of the day takes you through coastal dunes near the sea. Night in Leiden works well, a delightful small town.
- Leiden to Hague, 20 miles.
- Option:
  - Follow North Sea bike route to mouth of the Rhine River, then follow Rhine to Rotterdam, as provided in the Bikeline guide.
  - Alternatively, and recommended, ride from Hague to Delft, then to Gouda, 20 miles. Then into Rotterdam 15 miles. Note that some of this ride is on roads and not bike path, but it is a reasonably well-marked route and I think worth the extra navigation.
- Ride from Rotterdam to Dordrecht, 18 miles.
- Option
  - Follow Bikeline Guide Book Route:
    - Dordrecht to Von Gorinchem, 30 miles, good stop.
      - Option

- Take train from here to Utrecht and rejoin ride near Wijk Bij Duurstede, or ride to Wijk and then take detour from there to Utrecht.
  - Gorinchem to Geldermalsen, 29 miles
  - Geldermalsen to Wijk Bij Duurstede, 10 miles
  - Wijk Bij Duurstede to Rhenen, 20 miles
  - Rhenen to Arnhem, 21 miles
- **Recommendation**: I don't often recommend other routes over the routes in the Bikeline books, but I do here. I like the following route better:
  - Follow the Rhine out of Rotterdam, and at Kinderdikjk, and its wonderful windmills, follow the northern river along the Lek River.
  - Ride to Schoonhoven, an attractive town to stop, an old silver town. 46 miles.
    - Recommendation: The Hotel Belvedere is recommended, with good views and above-average breakfast.
  - Ride to Utrecht, spending a night in this interesting university town. 45 miles.
  - Ride Utrecht to Arnhem, 51 miles, or option to take train for all or part of this route, depending on schedule. This is a pleasant ride generally along the Nederrijin or Lower Rhine River, to Arnhem.
- Arnhem, the location of the famous Allied attempt to cross the Rhine river, portrayed in the film, "A Bridge Too Far." Interesting battlefields, museums and historic cemeteries.
  - Options. Arnhem War Museum and the Airborne Museum.
  - Recommendation: A visit to the fantastic Kroller-Muller Art Museum and park. The surrounding park is 5,500 hectares and is bike friendly. This makes a great short day ride from Arnhem, leaving luggage in your Arnhem hotel.
- Ride Arnhem to Millingen, 13 miles.
- Millingen to Kalkar, 17 miles.
  - Option:

Amsterdam to Rotterdam, Rhine to Frankfurt

- Overnight in small boarder city of Tolkamer— that is when there was a former border crossing between Holland and Germany.
  - Recommendation: Hotel Grand Cafe. www.detolkamar.nl. Built in 1905, located in Holland, but very close to German Border. Good restaurant.
  - Stop at Emmerich am Rhein
- Kalkar to Xanten, 13 miles (some shortcuts possible in this area).
- Xanten to Rheinberg. 15 miles.
- Rhienberg to Duisburg, 13 miles.
- At Kalkar, Xanten, or Duisburg, one suggestion is to take the train to Dusseldorf and skip this industrial segment. But riding is certainly possible. It depends on the amount of time you have and priorities. If you are looking for a segment to skip and save time, this quick train ride can save you more than a day riding.
- Spend the remainder of the day in Dusseldorf, and night in this interesting city, or head out and begin ride.
- Because it is possible to ride this route quickly, or at a slower pace, I will list a few of the more interesting places to visit and also spend the night. This route is easy to customize to whatever pace or distances are comfortable.
- Dusseldorf to Zons, 18 Miles. A nice small town and a potential stop on your first day if want a short day or started from Dusseldorf late in the day.
- Zons to Cologne, 16 Miles. Cologne is another great stop for a night, an interesting city to explore, being Germany's fourth largest city, and home to its famous cathedral.
- Cologne to Bonn, 19 Miles. Bonn is another interesting stop, the former capital of West Germany. It is a pleasant town to spend the night.
- Bonn to Remagen, 15 Miles. An interesting sightseeing stop, the site of a famous bridge over the Rhine that proved one of the most strategic targets late in WW2 as the last bridge left standing across the river. The bridge was captured by the Allies, and was

subject to a movie. Not recommended overnight given other options.

- Remagen to Bad Breisig, 4 Miles. A nice small town, and a good place for a stop to experience a smaller resort river town. Hotels and restaurants along the embankment, many with good views of the river.
  - o Recommendation: Hotel Anker along the river is a good buy with simple rooms, and restaurant downstairs.
  - o Note. If you would like to ride directly to Cochem up the Mosel, Bad Breisig makes a good stop, with a lunch stop in Koblenz before heading up the Mosel.
- Bad Breisig to Koblenz, 22 Miles. Another very good overnight stop, much to see in the city.
  - o Recommendation. In Koblenz, the Hotel Haus Morjan is good value and has rooms on the river with balconies. Nicer than our standard hotels, but three stars. Contact couple days ahead or more if can since can book up. www.Hotel-Morjan.de.
  - o Note. Koblenz is the turn-off for a ride up the Mosel.
- Koblenz to Wiesbaden, 54 Miles. This stretch provides many options. It can be completed in a day, especially if you use the many boats that cruise this area for part of the ride, such as 10-20 miles during a lunch break onboard. On the other hand, this section can take 3 days, taking ones time at the many charming towns that come one after another along this section of the river. There is probably no nicer section of small attractive towns along the entire Rhine. My advice is to take at least two days if you can, and enjoy.
- Here are some of the nicer towns along this stretch: Lahnstein, Braubach, Boppard, St. Goar, Oberwesel, Kaub, Bacharach, Lorch, Rudesheim, Bingen, Eltville. The last stretch from Rudesheim stay on the north bank of the river.
  - o Recommendation: Night at Oberwesel at one of my favorite hotels, **Auf Schonburg** (www.burghotel-schoenburg.de), a castle overlooking the Rhine, worth the higher price (inc. 4 course dinner) and climb!

Amsterdam to Rotterdam, Rhine to Frankfurt

- Several boats run this route many times a day. This provides an opportunity to ride boats for an hour for a coffee or lunch break, or gives some riders a chance to do more miles while other riders take a longer break. Consider taking a boat one direction and riding the other. A nice stretch to cruise is from St. Gore to Bacharach, which takes you passed the famous Lorelei Rock and the narrowest part of the river between Switzerland and the North Sea, and the inspiration for famous music and poems.
  - o Here are some boat lines:
    - www.k-d.com.
    - www.loreley-linie.de.
    - www.bingen-ruedesheimer.de.
    - www.rnf-schifffahrt.de.
  - o Recommendation:
    - Consider staying in Walluf near just west of Wiesbadan if looking for another stop. The hotel we liked was: the Zum Weissen Mohren.www.zum-weissen-mohren.de.   A good restaurant in town is Zum Treppchen.
    - Or stay in Mainz, other interesting cities to explore.
- Ride back to Frankfurt Airport and directly to hotel.
- From Eltville/Wiesbadan, stay on Rhine River until reach Main River, then head north.
- From Mainz cross Rhine River at north side of city heading to Kastel, then south on Rhine and turn onto Main River on north bank.
- Head toward Frankfurt.
- Cross Main River to south bank near Eddersheim or just before Sindlingen, head to Kelsterbach, get on the Kelsterbach Sud Road toward the airport and hotels. About 17 miles from Main/Rhine intersection to the Airport. About 3 miles from river to hotels at Airport, with bike lanes available almost entire way. Make sure you take the South Kelsterbach road to avoid traffic.

Dusseldorf (or Heidelberg) to Bodensee

Some longer distances on this route, three or four countries, so plenty to see and interesting stops, including Strasbourg and the Lake Bodensee:

Interesting: ****

Navigation: ***

Challenging: ***

Ride Highlights

Roundtrip flights in to Frankfurt and potential to rent bike.

Germany, France, Switzerland, and Austria.

Great boat infrastructure from Dusseldorf to Wiesbaden.

Good train infrastructure.

Great section of Rhine from Dusseldorf-Wiesbaden can be included, or repeated if toured before, or start south from Frankfurt.

Castles

Dusseldorf, Cologne, Bonn, Remagen (The Bridge Too Far), Koblenz

Heidelberg (short ride off the Rhine, or train ride).

Karlsruhe, Strasbourg, Colmar, Basel.

Rhine Falls at Schaffhausen.

Lake Bodensee

Dusseldorf (or Heidelberg) to Bodensee

Miles and Days

165 Miles from Dusseldorf to Mainz.
250 Miles from Mainz to Basel.
120 miles from Basel to Konstanz.
Full Ride (535 miles).
Shorter Ride (Starting at Heidelberg, 385 Miles).
This ride can be between 9-14 days, depending on use of trains to skip sections, side trips, and pace.

Esterbauer Book(s) Needed

Rhein-Radweg (2)
Rhein-Radweg (1)

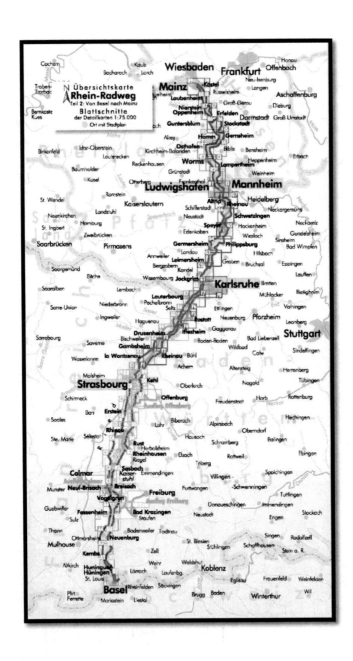

Dusseldorf (or Heidelberg) to Bodensee

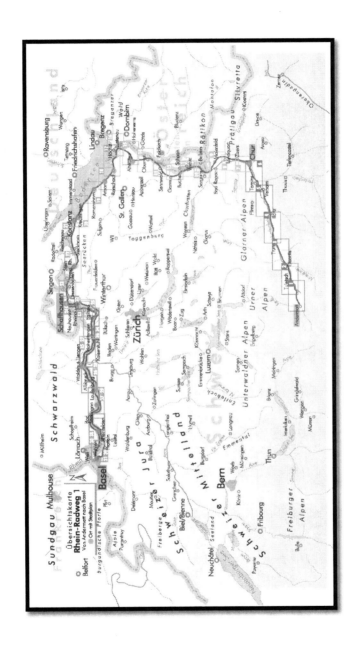

Cycling Along Europe's Rivers

Trail along the Rhine

Strasbourg

Dusseldorf (or Heidelberg) to Bodensee

Beautiful City of Colmar

Boat from Schaffhausen near Rhine Falls

Cycling Along Europe's Rivers

Ride Features

- Fly in and out of Frankfurt.
- Reserve the Sheraton, or other hotel near the airport for your last night and take your bike boxes to hotel after clearing customs upon arrival.
- Potential to rent a bike in Frankfurt, if so, take train to airport.
- Train to Dusseldorf
  - **Option.**
    - For shorter ride, take train to Heidelberg and spend your first night in Heidelberg.
    - Or can ride out of airport down the Main River to the Rhine River to Mainz, then head south on the Rhine following Bikeline Rhine-Radweg 2.

If starting in Dusseldorf:

- Spend the remainder of the day in Dusseldorf, and night, or head out and begin ride.
- Because it is possible to ride this route quickly, or at a slower pace, I will list a few of the more interesting places to visit and also spend the night. This route is easy to customize to whatever pace or distances are comfortable.
- Dusseldorf to Zons, 18 Miles. A nice small town and a potential stop on your first day if want a short day or started from Dusseldorf late in the day.
- Zons to Cologne, 16 Miles. Cologne is another great stop for a night, an interesting city to explore, being Germany's fourth largest city, and home to its famous cathedral.
- Cologne to Bonn, 19 Miles. Bonn is another interesting stop, the former capital of West Germany. It is a pleasant town to spend the night.
- Bonn to Remagen, 15 Miles. An sightseeing interesting stop, the location of a famous bridge over the Rhine that proved one of the most strategic targets late in WW2 as the last bridge left standing across the river. The bridge was captured by the Allies, and was

subject to a movie. Not recommended overnight compared to alternatives.

- Remagen to Bad Breisig, 4 Miles. A nice small town, and a good place for a stop to experience a smaller resort river town. Hotels and restaurants along the embankment, many with good views of the river.
  - o Recommendation: Hotel Anker along the river is a good buy with simple rooms, and restaurant downstairs.
  - o Note. If you would like to ride directly to Cochem up the Mosel, Bad Breisig makes a good stop, with a lunch stop in Koblenz before heading up the Mosel.
- Bad Breisig to Koblenz, 22 Miles.
  - o Recommendation.
    - Koblenz is very good overnight stop, much to see in the city. See it now, or after going up to Cochem, if you decide to ride that additional segment.
    - The Hotel Haus Morjan is good value and has rooms on the river with balconies. A bit nicer than our standard hotels, but three stars. Contact couple days ahead or more if can since can book up. www.Hotel-Morjan.de.
  - o Options:
    - Take a side trip up the Mosel River for a day. Ride to the medieval city Cochem, about 30 miles, including potential stop at Eltz Castle. Stay at the historic Alte Thorschenke hotel, with original buildings dating to 1332. www.castle-thorschenke.com.Consider booking ahead.
    - It is possible to take a boat back to Koblenz certain times of the year, take a train back, or ride back on Koblenz (or take the train back).
- Koblenz to Wiesbaden, 54 Miles. This stretch provides many options. It can be completed in a day, especially if you use the many boats that cruise this area for part of the ride, such as 10-20 miles during a lunch break onboard. On the other hand, this section can take 3 days, taking your time at the many charming

Cycling Along Europe's Rivers

towns that come one after another along this section of the river. There is probably no nicer section of small attractive towns along the entire Rhine. My advice is to take at least two days if you can, and enjoy.

- Here are some of the nicer towns along this stretch: Lahnstein, Braubach, Boppard, St. Goar, Oberwesel, Kaub, Bacharach, Lorch, Rudesheim, Bingen, Eltville. The last stretch from Rudesheim stay on the north bank of the river.
  - o Recommendation: Night at Oberwesel at one of my favorite hotels, **Auf Schonburg** (www.burghotel-schoenburg.de), a castle overlooking the Rhine, worth the higher price (inc. 4 course dinner) and climb!
- Several boats run this route many times a day. This provides an opportunity to ride boats for an hour for a coffee or lunch break, or gives some riders a chance to do more miles while other riders take a longer break. Even consider cruising one direction and riding the other. A nice stretch to cruise is from St. Gore to Bacharach, which takes you passed the famous Lorelei Rock and the narrowest part of the river between Switzerland and the North Sea, and the inspiration for famous music and poems.
  - o Here are some boat lines:
    - www.k-d.com.
    - www.loreley-linie.de.
    - www.bingen-ruedesheimer.de.
    - www.rnf-schifffahrt.de.
- Recommendation:
  - o Consider staying in Walluf near just west of Wiesbadan.
  - o The hotel we liked was the Zum Weissen Mohren.www.zum-weissen-mohren.de.
  - o A good restaurant in town is Zum Treppchen.
- Weisbaden to Mainz, 4 Miles.
- Ride from Mainz to Mannheim, with a potential stop in Worms. Total distance 44-60 miles.
  - o Option: Train from Wiesbaden or Mainz to Mannheim.
  - o Take a side trip up the Neckar River, Mannheim to Heidelberg 15 miles.

Dusseldorf (or Heidelberg) to Bodensee

- o Heidelberg is one of the special towns in Europe. It was never destroyed during WW2, it has retained its historic, albeit touristy, charm.
- Mannheim to Karlsruhe, 48 miles. From Heidelberg he ride is as much as 63 miles, but can take train part of the distance.
- Karlsruhe to Strasbourg, 50 miles. Strasbourg is a highlight of the ride, and a good place to stop for two nights, so you have a full day to explore the city and also take a break from the bike.
  - o Recommendation: See the Cathedral, climb the tower if you can for a great view. Tour the new buildings that are part of the core European Union government infrastructure. Consider doing the small boat river tour.
- Strasbourg to Colmar. Ride to Colmar along **the Canal Du Rhone au Rhine**, which starts just south west of the main hospital near Rue Humann. If you wanted to ride one of the canals of France, this is a great opportunity! Once on the trail (make sure you are on the right one given several routes) one of the easiest rides in the book. Straight with one turn to Colmar (47 miles). Options for side trips through some of the small wine towns along the route.
  - o Recommendation: Colmar is another highlight city of the ride. Consider the Hotel Le Rapp, well located near the old town and train station. Nicer 3 star hotel (reasonable for Colmar, 75E for single, 100E for double) that includes indoor pool. Good restaurant. www.rapp-hotel.com.
- Colmar back to Neuf-Brisach (11 Miles), then Neuf-Brisach to Basel (37 Miles).
  - o Option:
    - It is also possible to do a side trip to the beautiful city of Freiburg, leaving the route near Hartheim (18 miles each way).
    - Night in Basel.
- Basel to Laufenburg, 35 Miles, nice town to stop, or ride further this day.
- Laufenburg to Schaffhausen, 45 Miles. Or Rheinau.

- o **Highly Recommended**: The spectacular Rhine Falls, Rheinfall, are located between Neuhausen and Laufen-Uhwiesen, just south of Schaffhausen.
  - o Two miles past Schaffhausen descend right to the Falls at the Schloss Laufen. Boat rides available.
- Schaffhausen to Konstanz, 30 Miles.
  - o There are also boat options (expensive) to Konstanz along this route.
  - o Tour Lake Bodensee based on your schedule.
  - o Note: See the Lake Bodensee Ride for longer ride.
- Take train back to Frankfurt Airport after completing your tour of Lake Bodensee.
  - o Options:
    - It is also possible to ride to the eastern end of the Lake and train to Munich, and fly home from Munich.
    - Ride to Chur and consider riding near the beginning of the Rhine in the Alps -- take the train one-way if limited time.

Amsterdam to Lake Bodensee

A good mixture of sites and interesting cities, a variety of cultures, a bit more complicated than most other rides especially the first sections, but quite manageable:

Interesting: *****

Navigation: ***

Challenging: **

Ride Highlights

A Grand Trip, the Rhine River, from its mouth north of Rotterdam to Lake Bodensee.

Holland, Germany, France, Switzerland, and Austria.

Great boat infrastructure from Dusseldorf to Wiesbaden.

Good train infrastructure.

Flat well-marked route through bike friendly Holland.

Windmills and Cheese and Castles.

Amsterdam, Haarlan, Leiden, The Hague, Rotterdam (near the mouth of the Rhine), Utrecht.

Arnhem battleground and museums.

Dusseldorf, Cologne, Bonn, Remagen (The Bridge Too Far), Koblenz.

Heidelberg (short ride off the Rhine, or train ride).

Karlsruhe, Strasbourg, Colmar, Basel.

Rhine Falls at Schaffhausen and Lake Bodensee.

Additional ride possible to the mountains where the Rhine begins.

Cycling Along Europe's Rivers

Miles and Days

900 Miles
3 Weeks

Esterbauer Book(s) Needed

Rhein-Radweg (3)
Rhein-Radweg (2)
Rhein-Radweg (1)

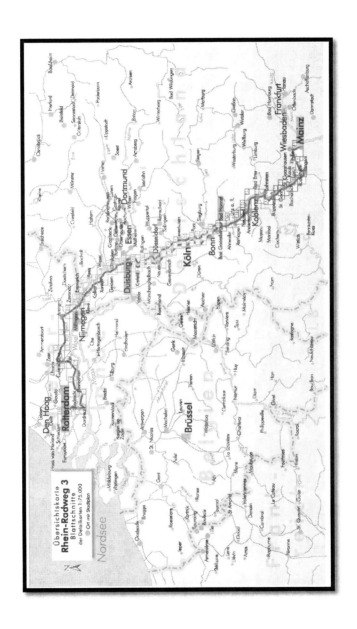

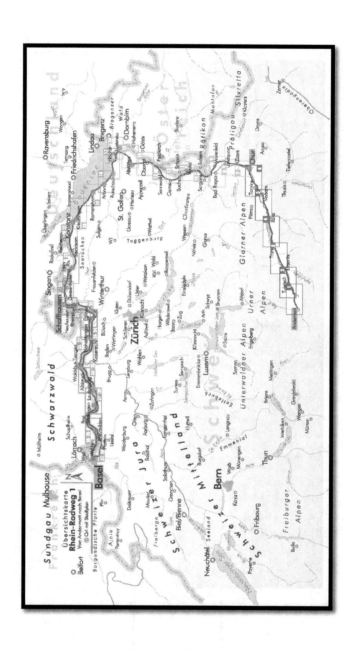

Amsterdam to Lake Bodensee

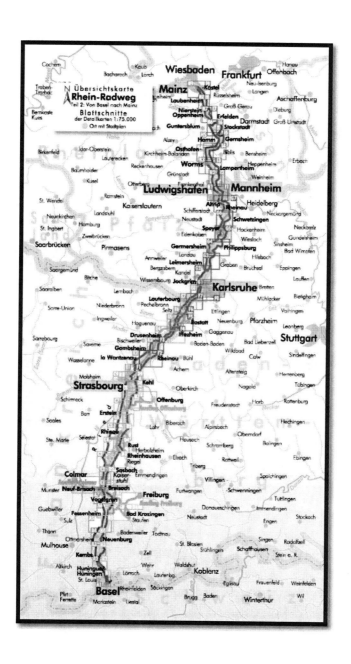

Boat on Rhine

Bad Breisig

Amsterdam to Lake Bodensee

Medieval Castle along Rhine Gorge

Rhine Falls

Cycling Along Europe's Rivers

Ride Features

- Fly into Amsterdam. This is a point-to-point ride, so need to mail your bike box to your destination in Frankfurt, for example the Sheraton hotel at the airport. You can also use disposable boxes furnished by airline, and usually possible to get a new box at Frankfurt airport (flight home will be from Frankfurt Airport or Munich Airport).
- Ride right out of the Amsterdam airport in this country with more bikes than the United States, and many well-marked bike trails.
- Option:
  - Head into Amsterdam and enjoy the city.
  - Start your ride and head toward Haarlen.
- Ride to Haarlen from Airport or Amsterdam, about 15 miles.
- Haarlen to Leiden, 18 miles by riding from Haarlem west to the North Sea, then follow the route until Katwijkaan Zee, then head south-east to Leiden. Most of the day takes you through coastal dunes near the sea. Night in Leiden works well, a delightful small town.
- Leiden to Hague, 20 miles.
  - Option:
    - Follow North Sea bike route to mouth of the Rhine River, then follow Rhine to Rotterdam, as provided in the Bikeline guide.
    - Recommendation: Ride from Hague to Delft, then to Gouda, 20 miles. Then into Rotterdam 15 miles. Note that some of this ride is on streets and not bike path, but it is a reasonably well-marked route and I think worth the extra navigation.
- Ride from Rotterdam to Dordrecht, 18 miles
- Option:
  - Follow Bikeline Guide Book Route:
    - Dordrecht to Von Gorinchem, 30 miles, good stop.
- Option:
  - Take train from here to Utrecht and rejoin ride near Wijk Bij Duurstede, or ride to Wijk and then take detour from there to Utrecht.

- - Gorinchem to Geldermalsen, 29 miles.
  - Geldermalsen to Wijk Bij Duurstede, 10 miles.
  - Wijk Bij Duurstede to Rhenen, 20 miles.
  - Rhenen to Arnhem, 21 miles.
  - o **Recommendation**: I don't often recommend other routes over the routes in the Bikeline books, but I do here. I like the following route better:
    - Follow the Rhine out of Rotterdam, and at Kinderdikjk, and its wonderful windmills, follow the northern river along the Lek River.
    - Ride to Schoonhoven, a very nice town to stop, an old silver town. 46 miles.
      - Recommendation: The Hotel Belvedere is recommended, with good views and above average breakfast.
    - Ride to Utrecht, spending a night in this interesting university town. 45 miles.
    - Ride Utrecht to Arnhem, 51 miles, or option to take train for all or part of this route, depending on schedule. This is a nice ride generally along the Nederrijin or Lower Rhine River, to Arnhem.
- Arnhem, the location of the famous Allied attempt to cross the Rhine river, portrayed in the film, "A Bridge Too Far." Interesting battlefields, museums and historic cemeteries.
  - o Options: Arnhem War Museum and the Airborne Museum.
  - o Recommendation: A visit to the fantastic Kroller-Muller Art Museum and park. The surrounding park is 5,500 hectares and is bike friendly. This makes a good short day ride from Arnhem, leaving luggage in Arnhem hotel.
- Ride Arnhem to Millingen, 13 miles.
- Millingen to Kalkar, 17 miles.
  - o Option:

Cycling Along Europe's Rivers

- o Overnight in small border city of Tolkamer— that is when there was a former border crossing between Holland and Germany.
  - Recommendation: Hotel Grand Cafe. www.detolkamar.nl. Built in 1905, located in Holland, but very close to German Border. Good restaurant.
  - o Stop at Emmerich am Rhein.
- Kalkar to Xanten, 13 miles (some shortcuts possible in this area).
- Xanten to Rheinberg. 15 miles.
- Rhienberg to Duisburg, 13 miles.
- At Kalkar, Xanten, Duisburg, one suggestion is to take the train to Dusseldorf and skip this industrial segment. But riding is certainly possible. It depends on the amount of time you have and priorities. If you are looking for a segment to skip and save time, this quick train ride can save you more than a day riding.
- Stay in Dusseldorf.
- Because it is possible to ride this next section to Wiesbaden quickly, or at a slower pace, I will list a few of the more interesting places to visit and also spend the night. This route is easy to customize to whatever pace or distances are comfortable.
- Dusseldorf to Zons, 18 Miles. A nice small town and a potential stop on your first day if want a short day or started from Dusseldorf late in the day.
- Zons to Cologne, 16 Miles. Cologne is another great stop for a night, an interesting city to explore, being Germany's fourth largest city, and home to its famous cathedral.
- Cologne to Bonn, 19 Miles. Bonn is another interesting stop, the former capital of West Germany. It is a pleasant town to spend the night.
- Bonn to Remagen, 15 Miles. An sightseeing interesting stop, the location of a famous bridge over the Rhine that proved one of the most strategic targets late in WW2 as the last bridge left standing across the river. The bridge was captured by the Allies, and was latter subject of a movie. Not recommended overnight compared to alternatives.
- Remagen to Bad Breisig, 4 Miles. A nice small town, and a good place for a stop to experience a smaller resort river town. Hotels

and restaurants along the embankment, many with good views of the river.

- o Recommendation: Hotel Anker along the river is a good buy with simple rooms, and restaurant downstairs.
- o Note. If you would like to ride directly to Cochem up the Mosel, Bad Breisig makes a good stop, with a lunch stop in Koblenz before heading up the Mosel.
- Bad Breisig to Koblenz, 22 Miles.
  - o Recommendation.
    - Koblenz is very good overnight stop, much to see in the city. See it now, or after going up to Cochem, if you decide to ride that additional segment.
    - The Hotel Haus Morjan is good value and rooms on the river with balconies. A bit nicer than our standard hotels, but three stars. Contact couple days ahead or more if can since can book up. www.Hotel-Morjan.de.
  - o Options:
    - Take a side trip up the Mosel River for a day. Ride to the medieval city Cochem, about 30 miles, including potentially the Eltz Castle. Stay at the historic Alte Thorschenke hotel, with original buildings dating to 1332. www.castle-thorschenke.com. Consider booking ahead.
    - It is possible to take a boat back to Koblenz certain times of the year, take a train back, or ride back on Koblenz (or take the train back).
- Koblenz to Wiesbaden, 54 Miles. This stretch provides many options. It can be completed in a day, especially if you use the many boats that cruise this area for part of the ride, such as 10-20 miles during a lunch break onboard. On the other hand, this section can take 3 days, taking your time at the many charming towns that come one after another along this section of the river. There is probably no nicer section of small attractive towns along the entire Rhine. My advice is to take at least two days if you can, and enjoy.

Cycling Along Europe's Rivers

- Here are some of the nicer towns along this stretch: Lahnstein, Braubach, Boppard, St. Goar, Oberwesel, Kaub, Bacharach, Lorch, Rudesheim, Bingen, Eltville. The last stretch from Rudesheim stay on the north bank of the river.
    - Recommendation: Night at Oberwesel at one of my favorite hotels, **Auf Schonburg** (www.burghotel-schoenburg.de), a castle overlooking the Rhine, worth the higher price (inc. 4 course dinner) and climb!
- Several boats run this route many times a day. This provides an opportunity to ride boats for an hour for a coffee or lunch break, or gives some riders a chance to do more miles while other riders take a longer break. Even consider cruising one direction and riding the other. A nice stretch to cruise is from St. Gore to Bacharach, which takes you passed the famous Lorelei Rock and the narrowest part of the river between Switzerland and the North Sea, and the inspiration for famous music and poems.
    - Here are some boat lines:
        - www.k-d.com.
        - www.loreley-linie.de.
        - www.bingen-ruedesheimer.de.
        - www.rnf-schifffahrt.de.
- Recommendation:
    - Consider staying in Walluf near just west of Wiesbadan.
    - The hotel we liked was: the Zum Weissen Mohren.www.zum-weissen-mohren.de.
    - A good restaurant in town is Zum Treppchen.
    - Weisbaden to Mainz, 4 Miles.
- Ride from Mainz to Mannheim, with a potential stop in Worms. Total distance 44-60 miles.
    - Option: Train from Wiesbaden or Mainz to Mannheim or all the way to Heidelberg.
    - Take a side trip up the Neckar River, Mannheim to Heidelberg 15 miles.
    - Heidelberg is one of the special towns in Europe. It was never destroyed during WW2, it has retained its historic, albeit touristy, charm.

- o Ride back along the Neckar too the Rhine River and continue south.
- Mannheim to Karlsruhe, 48 miles. From Heidelberg it is as much as 63 miles, but you can take trains part of the distance.
- Karlsruhe to Strasbourg, 50 miles. Strasbourg is a highlight of the ride, and a good place to stop for two nights, so you have a full day to explore the city and also take a break from the bike.
  - o Recommendation: See the Cathedral, climb the tower if you can for a great view. Tour the new buildings that are part of the core European Union government infrastructure. Consider doing the small boat river tour.
- Strasbourg to Colmar. Ride to Colmar along the **Canal Du Rhone au Rhine**, which starts just south west of the main hospital near Rue Humann. If you wanted to ride one of the canals of France, this is a great opportunity! Once on the trail (make sure you are on the right one given several routes) one of the easiest rides in the book. Straight with one turn to Colmar (47 miles). Options for side trips through some of the small wine towns along the route.
  - o Recommendation: Colmar is another highlight city of the ride. Consider the **Hotel Le Rapp**, well located near the old town and train station. Nicer 3 star hotel (reasonable for Colmar, 75E for single, 100E for double) that includes indoor pool. Good restaurant. www.rapp-hotel.com.
- Colmar back to Neuf-Brisach (11 Miles), then Neuf-Brisach to Basel (37 Miles).It is also possible to do a side trip to the beautiful city of Freiburg, leaving the route near Hartheim (18 miles each way). Night in Basel.
- Basel to Laufenburg, 35 Miles, fine town to stop, or ride further this day.
- Laufenburg to Schaffhausen, 45 Miles. Or Rheinau.
  - o **Highly Recommended**: The spectacular Rhine Falls, Rheinfall, are located between Neuhausen and Laufen-Uhwiesen, just south of Schaffhausen.
  - o Two miles past Schaffhausen descend right to the Falls at the Schloss Laufen. Boat rides available.
- Schaffhausen to Konstanz, 30 Miles.

Cycling Along Europe's Rivers

- There are also boat options to Konstanz along this route.
- Tour Lake Bodensee based on your schedule.
- Note: See the Lake Bodensee Ride for longer ride.
- Take train back to Frankfurt Airport after completing your tour of Lake Bodensee.
  - Options:
    - It is also possible to ride to the eastern end of the Lake and train to Munich, and fly home from Munich.
    - Ride to Chur and consider riding near the beginning of the Rhine in the Alps -- take the train one-way if limited time.

Lake Bodensee (Lake Constance)

Great first trip, easy day riding, a mixture of sites and recreation with the beautiful Lake, and even an opportunity for a downhill in the Alps. Great family route, including for non-riders --who can keep up with short ferry or train rides. **Easy local bike rental**.:

Interesting: ***

Navigation: *

Challenging: **

Ride Highlights

Four countries in a week! -- Germany, Switzerland, Austria, and Liechtenstein.

Easy touring, and very family and child friendly.

Local bikes can be rented at various towns.

Vacation atmosphere with beaches, boats, and holiday hotels. But the downside: more expensive area than typical trip, perhaps 20 percent higher overall, especially hotels. **Consider making hotel reservations for this trip June-September -- relatively crowded.**

Third largest lake in Central Europe 540 (square km), after Lake Geneva and Lake Balaton in Hungary. Formed during last Ice Age through the Rhine Glacier, it represents the widening of the Rhine River before moving to a narrow river heading to Basle.

Numerous cities and sites, over 270km of paved, hard packed, and small road trails.

Point-to-point riding, or pick a few hotels and take multi-day riding tours from each location without bags, making it a great tour to go on with non-riders.

Ferry/Rail system allows riders to move around the Lake.

Ride can be an add-on to a ride down the Rhine or the Danube.

Cycling Along Europe's Rivers

Miles and Days

More than 165 Miles.

4 -12 Days plus, depending on pace and other activities, given plenty of additional routes including Rhine Falls and Alps.

Esterbauer Book(s) Needed

Bodensee-Radweg
Rhein-Radweg 1, also useful

Lake Bodensee (Lake Constance)

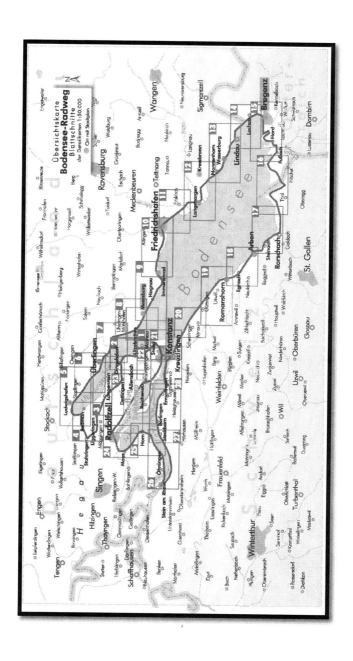

Cycling Along Europe's Rivers

Ride from Chur to Vaduz

Riding near Uberlingen

Lake Bodensee (Lake Constance)

View from Viva Sky in Konstanz

Lindau

Cycling Along Europe's Rivers

Ride Features

- Fly into Munich, Frankfurt, or Zurich. Zurich is the closest, under an hour train ride, or even cycle to Schaffhausen. Train from Munich Airport to Lindau through downtown, or from Frankfurt to Friedrichshafen or Konstanz. Both about three hours-plus trips.
- At Munich Airport, consider the great Kempinski Hotel -- convenient (roll 100 feet from lobby to check-in), comfortable, pool, and easy bike box drop off upon arrival. A bit expensive, and lower cost options also available near the airport.
- **Repair/Bike rental** (including E-Bikes) available in Lindau and Wasserburg (Unger -- www.fahrrad-unger.de), Bregenz (www.fahrradverleih-bregenz.at) and behind the Best Western, and in Konstanz.
- **More Good Bike Shops**: Radial, Inselgasse 13, Konstanz (Germany); Imholz, Wiesentalstrasse 135, Chur (Switzerland) ; CIC, Scholossergasse, Hochst (Austria).
- Touring can be point-to-point, moving from one town to another. In this case a circumnavigation works well, and 3-7 days is a reasonable period, but more days are fine.
- Alternatively, pick several attractive towns, stop for at least 2 nights in each, or fewer towns and more nights.
- I recently completed a 12 days trip in the area, and enjoyed many interesting routes, averaging about 30-35 miles per day.
- Take advantage of the elaborate ferry and rail systems to create many routes -- great flexibility on this ride.
- **There are many great routes in this area, but here are some suggestions:**
- Fly into Munich, train to Lindau, overnight in Lindau, Germany.
- Ride to Meersburg, about 33 miles, stopping in Friedrichshafen at the Zeppelin Museum. Langenargen is a nice smaller town stop, Consider the Hotel Seeterrasse. Climb tower at Schloss Montfort.
  - o In Meersburg, consider the Gasthof Zum Baren (www.baeren-meersburg.de), having served as a hotel/inn for 750 years, and owned by Michael Gilowsky's family for 150 years. Great restaurant, friendly, reasonable priced.

Lake Bodensee (Lake Constance)

No credit cards. A climb from the Lake, but then you are near the Old Castle.

- ○ Meersburg and Lindau are more tourist/souvenir towns.
- ○ Consider two nights here and day trip perhaps to Friedrichshafen, cross lake to Romanshorn, ride to Konstanz, and ferry back.

- Ferry to larger and interesting town of Konstanz (note the frequent car ferry drops you about 4 miles from central Konstanz). Spend 2/3 nights here, and day rides. Leave luggage in room!
  - ○ Consider the Viva Sky Hotel. Terrific views and rooftop restaurant/bar, very convenient to train station and downtown ferries. Good Indian restaurant across street.
  - ○ Ride to Schaffhausen, through the historic and beautiful, but touristy, Stein am Rhein. **Highly Recommended**: the truly incredible Rhine Falls. Two miles past Schaffhausen descend right to the Falls at the Schloss Laufen. Boat rides available. About 50 km one way -- ride back, train back, or take mid-afternoon boat (expensive) back to Konstanz.
  - ○ Loop from Konstanz to Meersburg, through Uberlingen (a potential stop, consider Hotel Seegarten or Hotel Seehof). Note that from Dingelsdorf to Bodman has hills, and can be avoided by ferry from Dingelsdorf to Uberlingen.
    - ▪ A **must stop** is the 45 hectare Mainau Island -- large botanic gardens, palace, butterfly center, restaurants, and amazing kids play area. Two-hours-plus should be allocated. www.mainau.de.

- Leave German Konstanz riding through Switzerland, to Austrian town of Bregenz (45 miles)-- 3 countries in a day! Most of the ride is good bike path, easier and generally better than German north side of Lake, but far less interesting. Overnight not recommended.
  - ○ Consider the well-located, convenient, and friendly Best Western Weisses Kreuz Hotel in this interesting city. Another option is the Deuring Schlossle Hotel, short climb, 17th century building, spacious rooms, nice views.
  - ○ The Pfanderbahn cable car ride is recommended, consider walking one-way if so inclined!

Cycling Along Europe's Rivers

- Bregenz to Chur, Swizterland -- ride one way, train (expensive) one way, with overnight in Liechtenstein capital of Vaduz. This is a valley, flat riding, flanked by mountains, with total elevation change under 300 feet -- pick your course based on wind direction.
    - Note that this region can be as much as 40 percent more expensive than nearby Germany -- trains, hotels, etc.
- Various beautiful routes available, but if you stay near the river (with some great dike riding along the crystal clear Rhine), about 34 miles from Bregnez to Vaduz and about 28 miles from Vaduz to Chur. Consider stops at Alstatten and medieval city of Feldkirch. Pay attention to trail just north of Landquart.
- Enjoy night at the splendid Park Hotel Sonnenhof in the 5,000 person capital city of Vaduz. Note it is a material climb, quite near to the castle, but worth the effort. Excellent Dinner! Great views and comfortable. Spa and pool. This area is not inexpensive, but good choice for nicer stay.
- In Chur, the friendly Hotel ABC (www.hotelabc.ch) makes a terrific multi-night stop, next to bike-friendly train station facilitating great day riding and excursions. Good breakfast, modern rooms, safe bike storage. Some Options:
    - Take 9 AM (2hr) train up to Oberalppass and ride down to Chur along the beginning Rhine River.
    - Day trip off the bikes on world-class train ride to St. Moritz (2 hrs each way), or a longer trip over the Alps to Poschiavo, or even to Italian town of Tirano (4 hrs each way).
    - Visit St. Moritz, and then on way back to Chur I understand there is a good ride from Preda to Thusis (about 40 km).
    - Also consider many splendid local hikes, including in the area from St. Moritz to Thusis.
- Stay at Bregnez or Lindau again after excursion up the Alps, then head back to Munich.
- **Option:** Potential to combine these rides with ride along the Danube starting at Danaueschingen or Ulm. About 25 miles from the north-west corner of the Lake to Danaueschingen, but some hills.

Danube River

The Danube River is another great Europe river that provides excellent cycling and touring opportunities. Originating in the small German town of Danaueschingen, the Danube flows 1,785 miles through Central and Eastern Europe to the Black Sea. Only the Volga River is longer than the Danube in Europe. Its journey takes it through 10 countries. Along the way it flows through Germany, Austria, Slovakia, and Hungary, the countries that will be the focus of this book. As the river continues, it also flows past Serbia, Bulgaria, Romania, Croatia, Ukraine, and Moldova. Like the Rhine, the Danube serves as a border between several nations. It also is a major transportation highway for shipping in these areas of Europe, with ocean going ships making it only to Romania, but river ships sailing well into Germany.

The completion of the Rhine-Main-Danube Canal, 171 km, in 1992, links the North Sea (and part of the Rhine River) to the Black Sea. (Note: This creates some additional route opportunities, not covered in this book.)

One of the other positive aspects of the Danube is that all the Bikeline books are in English!

Danube Headwaters (Danaueschingen)to Passau

Gives you a chance to see the beginning of the Danube as a small stream, interesting but lesser known cities, and a good addition to the Bodensee:

Interesting: ****

Navigation: **

Challenging: *

Ride Highlights

Fly Roundtrip into Frankfurt or Munich, with 3-4 hour train rides to get you to the ride and back from Frankfurt, and shorter train trip from Munich to Passau (1.5 hours).

Ride takes place in Germany.

Potential to combine with the Lake Bodensee ride. This provides for good variety in the ride, and also saves on train rides west.

Ride starts in the Black Forest and heads west as the Danube grows from a small stream to a river.

Beginning of the Danube at Danaueschingen.

Riedlinger, Ulm, Ingolstadt, Regensburg, Passau.

Danube Headwaters to Passau

Miles and Days

360 Miles from Danaueschingen to Passau
6-9 Days

Esterbauer Book(s) Needed

Danube Bike Trail (1) in English

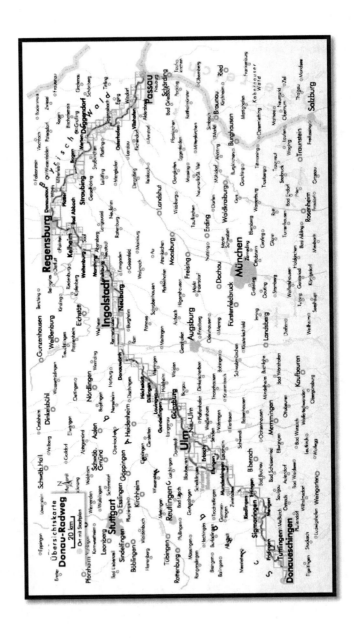

Danube Headwaters to Passau

Crossing from Lake Bodensee to Danube

Hills on the Crossing

The Beginning of the Danube

Riding along the Valley

Danube Headwaters to Passau

Schloss Sigmaringen

Riedlingen

Ulm from Top of Cathedral

Commercial Boat Traffic on Danube

Danube Headwaters to Passau

Bike Trail Ends, Boat Ride Begins

Boat from Weltenburg to Kelheim

Cycling Along Europe's Rivers

Ride Near Walhalla Temple

Early Morning Past Straubing

Danube Headwaters to Passau

Passau

Hotel Wilder-Mann Passau/Glass Museum/High Water Mark

Cycling Along Europe's Rivers

Ride Features

- Fly in to Frankfurt or Munich Roundtrip.
- At Munich Airport, consider the great Kempinski Hotel -- convenient (roll 100 feet from lobby to check-in), comfortable, and easy bike box drop off on arrival. A bit expensive, and lower cost options also near the airport.
- If Frankfurt, take train to Danaueschingen.
- If Munich, Options:
  - Can take the train from Munich to Danaueschingen.
  - Can take train to Lindau, and start your ride along the north side of Lake Bodensee.
    - Ride to the north-west section of the Lake, then can head north along small roads, some rolling hills, and a few steeper hills, to Danaueschingen (about 25 miles).
    - There is an option to take a train to Danaueschingen from Stockach (Wahlwies) (but it can be a 2 hour trip with 2 changes).
    - There is an option to train to Ulm, and a Bikeline book covers that route.
- There are many options for where to stop, making shorter or longer days possible:
  - Stop Options: Towns that make good stops include: Danaueschingen, Tuttlingen, Sigmaringen, Riedlingen, Munderkingen, Ehingen, Ulm, Gunzburg, Dillingen, Hochstadt, Danauworth, Neuburg, Ingolstadt, Kelheim.
  - The following is the route I have used.
- Danaueschingen to Tuttlingen, 25 Miles, short first day, or to Sigmaringen, 55 Miles.
- Tuttlingen (or Sigmaringen) to Riedlinger, 50 miles from Tuttlingen, or 20 Miles from Sigmaringen.
  - Option: Consider the Hotel Brucke in Sigmaringen. www.hotel-bruecke.de.
- Riedlinger to Ulm, 49 Miles.
- Ulm to Danauworth, 58 Miles.

Danube Headwaters to Passau

- Danauworth to Ingolstadt, 35 Miles.
- Ingolstadt to Regensburg, 52 Miles.
  - Option: Consider taking trains part of this route if need to save time.
  - Recommendation: One scenic part of this ride is the boat ride with bikes through the Danube Gorge, from Weltenburg to Kelheim. www.schiffahrt-kelheim.de.
- Regensburg to Straubing, 34 Miles.
  - Options:
    - See the Temple built by King Ludwig 1, Walhalla, on this route, climb up for a great view.
- Straubing to Passau, 55 Miles.
  - Option: Can take boat from Deggendorf to Vilshofen for a break.
  - Consider two nights in Passau, especially if arriving later in the day. It is a great town to explore.
    - Recommendation: The Hotel Wilder Mann in Passau is an historic hotel in the center of town, also housing a glass museum. Well-priced for the historic atmosphere and location. Simple accommodations. www.wilder-mann.com.
  - Day Ride Option:
    - Take a day ride to Engelhartszell 32 Miles (leaving luggage at hotel in Passau), take boat back to Passau.
  - Longer Ride Option:
    - Continue on the Danube toward Vienna.
  - If finished, train back to Munich.
- Danube-Bodensese Bike Route Option:
  - Esterbauer Book: Danube-Bodensese Radweg.
  - There are several routes connecting the Danube and Lake Bodensee, including from Riedlingen or Ulm on the Danube, and the northern shore of the Lake.
  - Many of these routes involve hills on a regular basis.

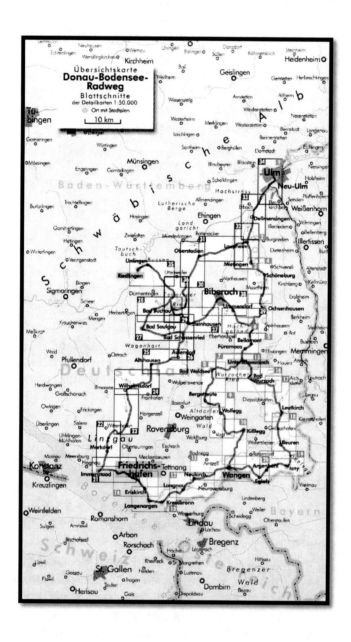

Salzburg to Passau Option

A short addition that takes you through smaller rivers, less traveled, with Salzburg as a highlight:

Interesting: ***

Navigation: **

Challenging: ***

Ride Highlights

Good addition to Danube Ride.

Visit the beautiful city of Salzburg.

Ride smaller Inn River and Salzach River.

Castle at Burghausen.

Small Towns.

Miles and Days

87 Miles from Salzburg to Passau.
Longer routes available if start in Krimml, total 185 Mile to Passau.

Esterbauer Book(s) Needed

Tauern- Radweg

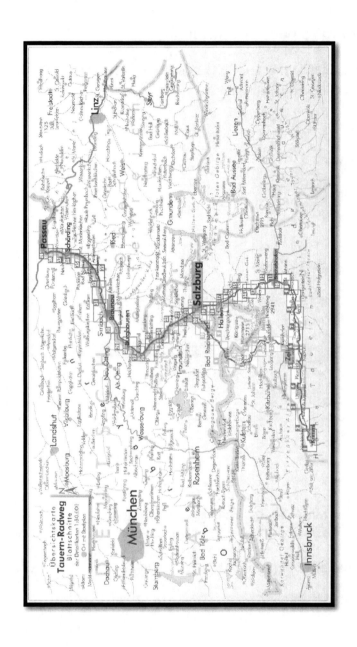

Salzburg to Passau

Salzburg Castle

View from Salzburg Castle

Cycling Along Europe's Rivers

Along the Inn and Salzach River

Along the Inn and Salzach River

Salzburg to Passau

Ride Features

- Fly into Munich, and take train to Salzburg.
  - Options: It is also possible to get a van and driver to take you if you have the budget, which will save you considerable time.
- At Munich Airport, consider the great Kempinski Hotel -- convenient (roll 100 feet from lobby to check-in), comfortable, and easy bike box drop off on arrival. A bit expensive, and lower cost options also near the airport.
- Spend the night in the wonderful city of Salzburg.
- Head out on the Salzach River.
- Salzburg to Burghausen. 32 Miles. Visit its imposing Castle. Overnight.
- Continue on the Salzach River where it soon merges with the Inn River a few miles before Braunau.
  - Note: It is also possible to spend the night in Braunau, which is worth a stop to see the memorial to the victims of WW2 in front of the building where Hitler was born.
- Burghausen to Passau. 54 Miles.

Innsbruck to Passau Option

Good addition to Danube, and gives you some downhill and a chance to see Innsbruck, but a bit more complicated logistics:

Interesting: ***

Navigation: **

Challenging: ***

Ride Highlights

Good addition to Danube Ride.

Alternative to Salzburg Ride.

Ride on the Inn River.

Mostly Downhill from Innsbruck.

Mountain Scenery.

Sand and Gravel paths, as well as paved.

I have not undertaken the section between Innsbruck to Braunau, so will not provide details for this route.

Innsbruck to Passau

Miles and Days

190 Miles from Innsbruck to Passau

Esterbauer Book(s) Needed

Inn-Radweg 2

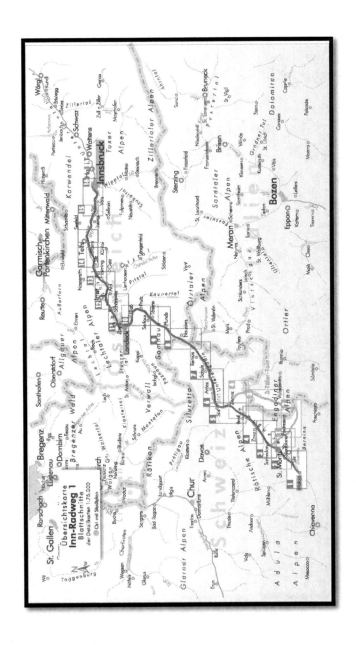

Passau to Vienna

One of my favorite routes in the book, along with the Rhine Gorge (Dusseldorf to Wiesbaden), easy, interesting, beautiful, varied:

Interesting: *****

Navigation: *

Challenging: *

Ride Highlights

Recommended: This is one of the great stretches of the Danube, and one of the easiest rides in Europe.

Ride starts in Germany, but mostly takes place in Austria.

Trails are well-marked, and often are available on both sides of the river.

Bikeline books in English.

Most trails stay very close to the river.

Great towns to stop along the way, and good rail infrastructure.

Boats on many sections.

Passau, Aschach, Linz, Mauthausen, Grein, Melk, Durnstein, Krems, Vienna.

Cycling Along Europe's Rivers

Miles and Days

200 Miles
4 to 6 Days

Esterbauer Book(s) Needed

Danube Bike Trail 2 — in English

Passau to Vienna

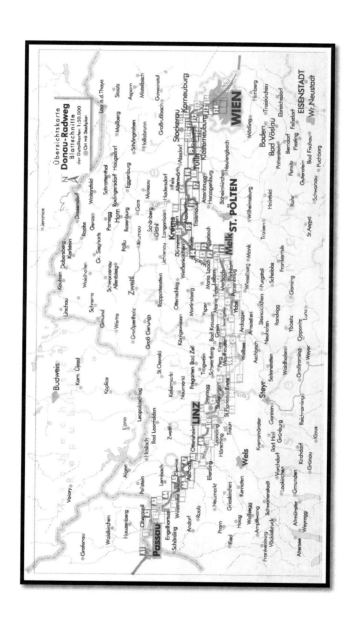

Cycling Along Europe's Rivers

Danube with Dam in Background that Serves as Bike Crossing

Along the Danube

Passau to Vienna

Castle in Background

From Balcony at Hotel Faust Schloss in Aschach

Mauthausen Concentration Camp

Mauthausen Concentration Camp Memorial

Passau to Vienna

Entering Grein

Ferry in Grein

Cycling Along Europe's Rivers

Along the River

A Few Times the Trail is not Paved, Like This Farm Road

Passau to Vienna

Trail Through the Fields

View from Melk Cathedral

Cycling Along Europe's Rivers

Melk

Beautiful Wachau Valley

Passau to Vienna

Wachau Valley

Pool at Hotel Richard Lowenherz in Durnstein

Castle on River Past Melk

Passau to Vienna

Ride Features

- Fly into Munich.
    - Options: Can return from Munich by taking train, or even boat.
    - Alternatively, fly home from Vienna, and send bikes boxes to a hotel near Vienna airport you have reserved in advance.
    - Taking train back to Munich for RT is likely easiest solution.
- At Munich Airport, consider the great Kempinski Hotel -- convenient (roll 100 feet from lobby to check-in), comfortable, and easy bike box drop off on arrival. A bit expensive, and lower cost options also near the airport.
- Can ride from Munich airport to Freising or other nearby town to catch train to Passau (bit more complicated but saves time), or take train from airport into central Munich and catch train from Munich to Passau.
- Worth a night in Passau upon arrival if you have the time. It is possible to take a good warm-up ride along the Inn or Ilz Rivers if staying in Passau (I recommend the Inn River starting near the Marienbrucke). Passau is situated where three rivers intersect: Danube, Inn, Ilz Rivers.
    - Recommendation: The Hotel Wilder Mann in Passau is an historic hotel in the center of town, also housing a glass museum. Well-priced for the historical atmosphere and location. Simple accommodations. www.wilder-mann.com.
    - Note: When setting off on the Danube, make sure you take the correct river, it can be confusing. Go across the Luitpoldbrucke, crossing the Danube from the main town, then quickly across the Neuellzbrucke and start along the northern side of the Danube.
    - Recommendation: Keep the boat system in mind on your trip, given that boats can run, with various routes, from Passau all the way to Vienna. Linz is often a stop in the middle of the routes. Use the boats for

short hops for a break or to let one rider go further some days. Also, you can even ride one-way to Vienna, and take boats back, a nice way to do the roundtrip if flying in and out of Munich. Here are some of the boat companies:
- www.donauschiffahrt.de.
- www.brandner.at.
- www.donauschiffahrt-wurm.de

- Passau to Aschach, 44 Miles. At Jochenstein continue on the northern side of river, unless you would like to visit the interesting stop at Engelhartszell.
  - Recommendation:
    - In Aschach, stay at the Hotel Faust Schloss, relatively not too expensive, great views and good restaurant. One of my favorite hotels on the rivers, and have stayed there a few times. It is located on the north side of the river, across from the main town. Getting to the hotel involves a bit of a climb up the driveway, so once there, you might not want to come back down until the morning! Have dinner at the beautiful terrace restaurant. There is a ferry just before Aschach you can take across the river if it is running, or at end of the town cross the bridge.
- Aschach to Grien. 54 Miles. In Grein consider the Goldenes Kreuz Hotel, simple rooms, good location, cycle friendly, hospitable.www.hotel-in-grein.at.
  - Options:
    - This ride can be broken into two days at several attractive towns.
    - Recommendation: About 32 Miles from Aschach is Mauthausen, one of the notorious concentration camps from WW2 in Austria. It has a fine museum, and is quite a moving experience. It is a short ride (uphill) from the north bank of the river.

- The stretch after Mauthausenis short of stops, so bring a snack/water.
- In Grien, check out the beer and snack spot along the river.
- Grien to Durnstein. 43 Miles. Head out of Grein by crossing on ferry and ride on southern side of Danube. Take a break at Pochlarn, or go all the way to Melk. After Melk, cross over to the northern side of the Danube at Emmersdorf and head north-east along the river. Great stretch ahead!
  - Recommendations:
    - A stop in Melk to visit the magnificent Benedictine Abby.
    - Ride through the Wachau Valley, one of Austria's most beautiful wine areas.
    - Special Recommendation: Night at the Hotel Richard Lowenherz, sleep where Richard the Lionheart spent time during his crusade travels. More expensive than most recommended in this book, but worth if can get a reasonable price. Nice pool and historic.
    - Consider taking the boat with your bike for part of this ride today. Get lunch or a snack on board!
- Durnstein to Vienna, 60 Miles.
  - Can take train part of this route. For example, train from Krems to Absdorf-Hippersdorf, change for Vienna, total about 90 minutes point to point. Depends on your timing and priorities. If I had to skip one segment on this route, I would train from Krems to Vienna. If time, ride the full way.
- Vienna
  - Options:
    - Spend 2-3 nights in this very interesting city.
    - Options:
      - Fly home from here.
      - Train back to Munich.

Cycling Along Europe's Rivers

- Boat back to Passau, then train to Munich (or ride partway if have time).
- Consider a day ride to Bratislava, Slovakia, about 44 Miles.
  - Can be a day ride, leaving your luggage in Vienna.
  - Ride to Bratislava and spend a night in this interesting town, or take the train back to Vienna.
- Consider additional ride to Budapest.

Vienna to Budapest

Very enjoyable ride, combining two of Europe's great cities, and three countries, but a bit more challenging navigation than most trips and you can go a day only seeing a couple riders (which is fun but also you are out there a bit more):

Interesting: *****

Navigation: ***

Challenging: **

Ride Highlights

Ride in Austria, Slovakia, Hungary.

Can combine with ride from Passau for longer trip.

Large cultural cities and smaller towns.

Ok train support system, but not like other parts of the Danube in Austria or the Rhine.

Ride along the river in many areas, but also off the river in areas, especially the first half of the ride in Hungary.

A bit more complicated than first part of the Danube, so more route information is provided herein.

Vienna, Bratislava, Gyor, Tata, Esztergom, Szentendre, Budapest.

Miles and Days

185 Miles

5 Days

Esterbauer Book(s) Needed

Danube Bike Trail (3)— in English

Vienna to Budapest

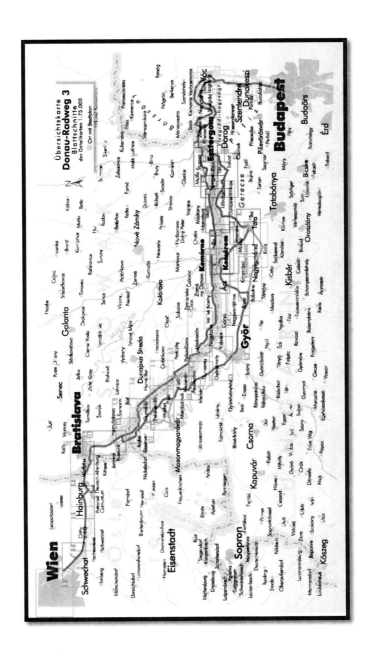

Trail between Vienna and Bratislava

Vienna to Budapest

Entering Bratislava

Botel Gracia (Hotel) Bratislava

Crossing Border from Slovakia to Hungary

Market in Gyor

Vienna to Budapest

Casablanca Hotel Tata

Lake at Tata

Cycling Along Europe's Rivers

Riding Back in Slovakia

Crossing back from Slovakia to Hungary

Vienna to Budapest

Esztergom on Danube Bend

View from Esztergom

Cycling Along Europe's Rivers

Small Ferry Crossing Outside Budapest

Budapest

Vienna to Budapest

Ride Features

- Fly into Vienna.
  - Options:
    - Fly home from Vienna, and leave bike box at hotel you have reserved for your last night before flying home, a hotel near the Vienna airport.
      - Take train back to Vienna. Not a bad option since under 3 hour train ride. Need to confirm trains that can carry bikes.
    - Fly home from Budapest, mail your box to a hotel near the airport in Budapest you have reserved ahead for your last night.
- Vienna to Bratislava, Slovakia, 44 Miles. Easy ride, not as scenic as ride from Passau to Vienna.
  - Option: Stay in a boat hotel, the Botel Gracia, for a different experience and good price. www.hotelgracia.sk.
- From here, toward Budapest, there are bike routes on both sides of the Danube, but I think the southern side (Hungarian Side) is more interesting until Komarom.
- Bratislava to Gyor, 52 Miles. This ride is through some very quiet areas, parts of Hungary that were near the border with the west and have been lefts somewhat behind in time. The ride even takes you over some of these old now dismantled border areas.
  - Recommendation:
    - In Gyor, Hotel Klastrom, a converted monastery, now makes an interesting and well-priced stay in town. www.klastrom.hu.
    - Visit the old Synagogue that is converted into an art gallery.
- Gyor to Tata, 38 Miles. For this route there is a more direct road (than outlined in the Bikeline guide) that is not bad for

riding, but not a bike trail, from Gyor to Tata, making the route 38 Miles. Just follow the road signs to Tata. You can also follow the Bikeline guide and ride through Komarom to Tata, increasing the miles to near 45.Given that you will go back through Komarom on the route recommended herein, I would consider the shorter route here, which would leave you more time in the lovely town of Tata.

- o Recommendation:
  - In Tata, the Hotel Casablanca, a large historic house right on the lake with great views and good point for exploring. Try and get a room with a view!www.hotels.hu/casablanca.
  - Try and spend at least a half a day walking around Tata and its beautiful lake, so get an early start from Gyor.
- Tata to Esztergom, 50 Miles. Ride back from Tata to Komarom, about 11 Miles, then over the bridge into Slovakia and through the nicer town of Komarno. Then follow the trail on the Slovakia side of the Danube, giving you time in another country and a better route. Stop in Moca for a break since it is hard to find refreshments along parts of this quiet route. At Storovo cross the bridge into the beautiful city of Esztergom.
  - o Recommendation:
    - Get a photo with your group on the bridge over the Danube as you cross into Esztergom.
    - Walk up to the Basilica and enjoy the views.
    - Hotel Esztergom near the entrance to the city is convenient and a good value, although quite ordinary.www.hotel-esztergom.hu.
- Esztergom to Szentendre, 40 Miles. About 6 miles after Esztergom take a left and go toward ferry that takes you across Danube to Szob, if working (which it often is not.) If miss this turnoff, just past Domos there is another ferry across, if working. If no ferries working, continue to Visegrad and cross there to Nagymaros. Have lunch in Vac. Cross Danube using ferry at Vic and ride to Tahitofalu on this island, about 2 miles. Take left at Tahitofalu (do not cross river again

there), and ride the quiet stretch to Szigetmonostor, at the end of the island, where you will cross the river by ferry. Ride into Szentendre, a nice small town to explore before entering Budapest.

- o Option: Consider staying at the Centrum Panzio hotel, www.hotelcentrum.hu, very simple rooms but good price, located right next to river.
- Szentendre to Budapest, 17 Miles. An interesting, although increasingly busy, ride into a large town, with impressive views as the city finally appears.
  - o Recommendation:
    - Spend at least a full day in this fascinating and beautiful city of Budapest.
    - Hotel Victoria provides good views and value in this more expensive city. A somewhat higher level than our standard hotel, 4 stars. www.victoria.hu.
    - Consider the Hop On and Off bus tours to see much of the city in a compressed time period.
    - If flying out from the airport, consider Hotel Stacio near the Budapest airport. www.hotelstacio.hu.
- Extension Options:
  - o Continue ride to the Croatia border using the Bikeline Danube Bike Trail 4. The ride through the remainder of Hungary is about 120 Miles.
  - o Take an excursion, by riding, or by train (one way or both ways) to Lake Balaton and enjoy its terrific cycling routes.

Budapest to Black Sea along the Danube

I have not done this one, but looks great if you have the time and the conditioning:

Interesting: *****

Navigation: *****

Challenging: *****

Ride Highlights

A grand tour through multiple countries.

Budapest

Baja

Vukovar

Novi Sad

Belgrade

Derlap National Park and the Danube Gorge.

Drabeta-Turnu Severin.

Bucharest (off the main route)

Constanta on the Black Sea.

Castles and Ruins.

Black Sea

Budapest to Black Sea along the Danube

Miles and Days

960 Miles
3 plus weeks

Esterbauer Book(s) Needed

Danube Bike Trail (4)— in English
- Note: This one book covers 960 miles, much more than a standard Bikeline book. That means the maps provide considerably less detail than standard Bikeline books.

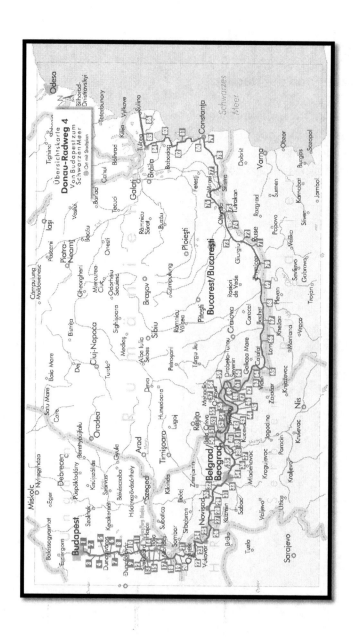

Budapest to Black Sea along the Danube

Ride Features

- Note: I have not attempted this ride for a variety of reasons (some listed below), but it looks fascinating if you have the time and fitness.
- The first section looks the easiest, and could be a good addition for a ride from Vienna to Budapest.
- General issues to consider about this route:
    - On roads quite often, rather than bike trails.
    - Away from river often.
    - Much less flat than standard rides— this is not one of the low climbing routes that are the focus of this book.
    - Less infrastructure support, including less rail support. You are out there on your own more than other rides in this book.
    - Good news: Lower per day costs.

Danube Combination Routes

There are many different combinations along the Danube from the headwaters through Budapest. Here are a few ideas:

- **Passau to Budapest**
    - Passau to Krems, then train to Vienna or Bratislava, then ride to Budapest.
    - Options:
        - The ride from Krems to Bratislava is fine, but not that interesting, so not a bad segment to skip if short on time.
        - Ride this section if have time so can see Vienna.
        - If limited time, try and stop at Vienna by train for a visit.
    - Roundtrip air flights into Vienna.
- **Melk to Budapest**
    - Roundtrip air fights into Vienna.
- **Beginning of Danube to Vienna**
    - Danaueschingen, Ulm, or Regensburg to Vienna.
        - Fly into Munich, home from Vienna, or Roundtrip into Munich and train back from Vienna.
- **Good Extensions**
    - **Passau to Prague**
        - Passau to Prague and Ceske Krumlov using the Moldau-Radweg. The connection is near Obermuhl before Aschach. See the Bikeline book for this route.
    - **Lake Bodensee**
        - Add some riding around Lake Bodensee.
    - **Lake Balton**
        - Add some riding around Lake Balton.

Elbe River

The Elbe River is the last of Europe's major rivers covered in this book. The Elbe flows 680 miles from the Czech Republic through Germany, past Prague, Dresden, and Hamburg to the North Sea at Cuxhaven.

A fine bike trail runs the course of the river, and the two Elbe Bikeline books are in English.

Route Direction Note: Given the generally westerly winds, the best odds of avoiding a strong headwind is to ride from the north-west to the south-east. This can be a bit confusing since the Bikeline books follow the opposite direction. The good news is after a few minutes getting used to working a bit backward, it becomes much easier. The books also have text that assists with the route direction recommended herein. It is useful to have one larger independent map of the region to use with the Bikeline books to assist given that you are going in the opposite direction laid out in the guides.

Hamburg to Prague

This ride that takes you between two of Europe's interesting major cities (Hamburg and Prague), with other interesting sites along the way, but not as interesting as middle of Danube or Rhine, for example:

Interesting: ****

Navigation: ***

Challenging: **

Ride Highlights

Visit Germany, including areas that were formerly in East Germany, and the Czech Republic.

Small towns and large cities.

Good rail infrastructure in parts of this ride, and also areas with not as good coverage.

Boats available on segments.

North Sea at Cuxhaven option.

Stade, Hamburg, Magdeburg, Wittenberg, Meissen, Prague, Dresden.

Hamburg to Prague

Miles and Days

300 Miles from Cuxhaven to Magdeburg.
205 Miles from Hamburg to Magdeburg.
300 Miles from Magdeburg to Prague.
10 Plus days, but sections can be skipped by train to shorten route.

Esterbauer Book(s) Needed

Elbe River Trail (1) English
Elbe River Trail (2) English

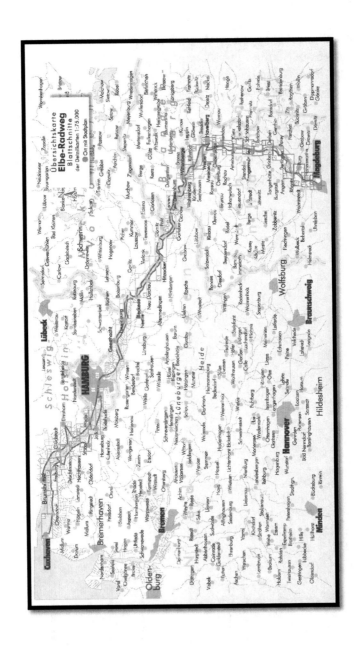

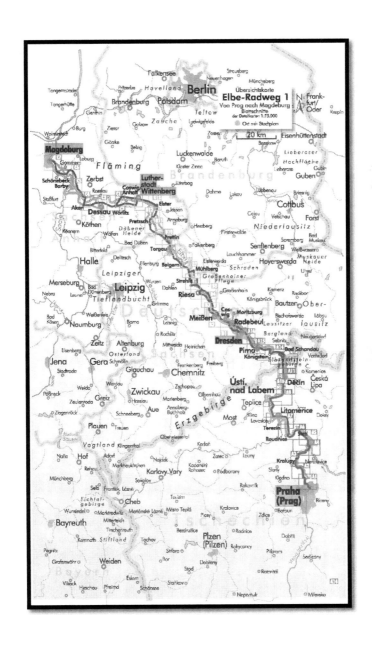

Wittenberg

Hamburg to Prague

Bikes on Ferry

Rural Trail

Meissen with Ferry Boat

Outside Meissen

Hamburg to Prague

Entering Dresden by Boat

Boat from Dresden to Pillnitz Castle

Cycling Along Europe's Rivers

Quiet Trail as Approach Former German-Czech Boarder

Quiet Trail as Approach Former German-Czech Boarder

Hamburg to Prague

Rough Trail

Decin

Terezin Ghetto Cemetery

Litomerice, near Former Terezin Ghetto

Hamburg to Prague

Castle at Melnik

Elbe and Moldau Split

Cycling Along Europe's Rivers

Prague

Ride Features

- Flight Options:
    - Roundtrip Hamburg Option:
        - Fly roundtrip into Hamburg. Upon arrival, leave bike boxes at hotel near the airport that you have reserved ahead, such as the Mercure near Hamburg Airport.
        - Can take train from end of trip back to Hamburg, such as from Prague. Note that it will be a long train back since will need to use special bike trains. Check train schedules before choosing this option.
    - Fly into Hamburg/ home from Prague Option:
        - Reserve hotel near Prague airport ahead of time, and mail box to the hotel from Hamburg airport.

Hamburg to Prague

- I recommend shipping box and flying back from Prague, avoiding long train back to Hamburg.
- From airport, ride to center of Hamburg, or take the train from the airport.
  - Options:
    - Extension Options. If doing one of the extension options, north or west, as described below, then take train there today.
    - If heading to Prague, then spend a night in Hamburg, a very interesting city to explore and cycle.
  - Head down the trail toward Prague.
  - Hamburg to Lauenburg. 32 Miles.
  - Lauenburg to Hitzacker. 22 Miles.
  - Option: Ride from Hamburg to Hitzacker 54 Miles .
  - Hitzacker to Wittenberge. 47 Miles. Spend night.
  - Wittenberge to Tangermunde. 52 Miles. Spend night.
  - Tangermunde to Magdeburg. 44 Miles. Spend night.
  - Magdeburg to Wittenberg 61 Miles.
  - Recommendation: Wittenberg has much to explore, including the church that was the site of Luther's 95 Theses. Consider staying at the Luther-Hotel Wittenberg. www.luther-hotel-wittenberg.de.
  - Shorter Ride Option:
    - Spend a night at Dessau (43 Miles), or take train from Dessau to Wittenberg (about 35 minute train ride that runs often).
  - **Berlin Extension Option**: There is the option to ride from here to Berlin, or take the train part of the way and ride into Berlin, see the Berlin Option, further in the book.
    - Wittenberg to Torgau. 50 Miles.
      - Consider the Central-Hotel Torgau. Good location built in 1908.www.central-hotel-torgau.de.
    - Torgau to Dresden. 59 Miles. Explore Dresden, at least a half day. Not a bad city for two nights so there is a full day to explore.
  - Recommendation.

- If time, consider a boat trip to nearby Schloss Pillnitz for a river boat experience and chance to explore. Some of these boats are quite historic on this route. www.saechsische-dampfschiffahrt.de/index-en.html.
- Consider the Hotel Rothenburger Hof, good location and even a small pool.

o Shorter Ride Option:
  - Stop at Meissen for the night, about 44 Miles from Torgau.
  - Meissen makes an interesting break on the trip, with its famous porcelain industry and interesting streets.
  - A stop for the night here would allow you to get into Dresden early to have most of the day to explore this larger city. Meissen to Dresden. 15 Miles.

o Recommendation:
  - Consider boats that run from Dresden to Meissen, and down to Decin on some dates. Some of these boats are quite historic, including the oldest fleet of paddle steamers in the world.
    www.saechsische-dampfschiffahrt.de/index-en.html.
  - Dresden to Decin. 48 Miles.
    - Decin makes a good stop. Consider the Hotel Ceska Koruna. www.hotelceskakoruna.xz.
  - Decin to Litomerice. 32 Miles.

o Recommendation.
  - Ride to the Terezin Ghetto outside of Litomerice (leave your bags at your hotel in Litomerice). Allow a few hours for this very interesting and moving visit. The camp was part of a Nazi PR program to show the world that things were not that bad in the camps generally, and was portrayed as a "self-governed Jewish settlement area."
  - Litomerice to Prague. 55 Miles. There are a few small towns to stop along this route if you wish to break up this long day, including a stop in Melnik, or take the train for a short hop, such as from Melnik to Prague.

o Recommendation:

- If you need a break, consider a Thai massage and meal, and even a stop, in Rez u Prahy, about 6 miles from Prague on the road north. An unexpected find! www.allthai.cz.
- It is possible to stay at the nearby Hotel Vltava with its simple accommodations, about $50 per night.
- This stop can be useful if you are getting to Prague late, and also want to take a break. Save money on a Prague hotel — stay here, have a massage and Thai dinner, then head into Prague early for a full day, with only one night in the more expensive hotels in Prague.
- Spend at least a full day in Prague, much to explore.
- **Extension Options:**
  - Consider the Cesky Krumlov Extension, as described below.
  - Potential to ride Greenway to Vienna.

Cesky Krumlov (Passau/Vienna) Moldau Option

Cresky Krumolov is a terrific small town and five stars alone, the rest of the ride is more challenging but a good addition, although the challenging segments can be skipped using trains, and Cresky enjoyed:

Interesting: ***

Navigation: ***

Challenging: ****

Ride Highlights

Good addition to a ride on the Elbe or the Danube Rivers.

Train from Prague, or even start in Passau or on Danube River.

Cesky Krumlov: A UNESCO World Heritage City, one of the most scenic cities covered in this book.

Smaller, scenic, Czech towns and countryside.

Route options.

Ride to Lipno Lake.

Potential Hills on part of route.

Cesky Krumlov Moldau River

Miles and Days

Multiple Options
245 Miles from Passau to Prague.
210 Miles from Danube River to Prague.
146 Miles from Cresky Krumlov to Prague.
46 Mile day ride from Cresky Krumlov to Horni Lana, and 23 Mile ride from CK to Budejvice.

Esterbauer Book(s) Needed

Moldau- Radweg

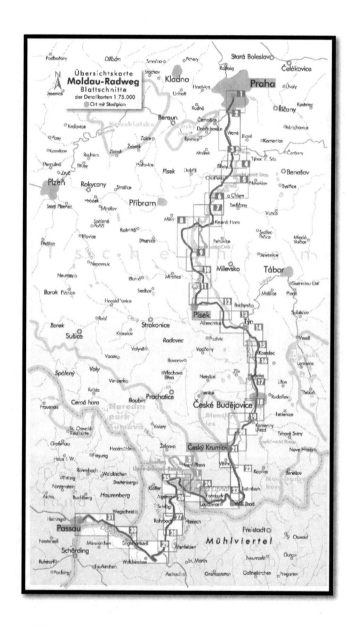

Cesky Krumlov Moldau River

Cresky Krumlov

Cresky Krumlov

Cresky Krumlov

Cresky Krumlov

Ride along the Vltava (or Moldau) River South

Cycling Along Europe's Rivers

Ride Features

o This is an extension south of Prague.
o Options:
  - From Prague: Take train to Cresky Krumlov from Prague, and commence ride at that point.
  - From Passau: Consider flying into Munich, taking train to Passau, and commencing ride at that point.
    - 32 Miles from Passau to Von Obermuhl.
    - Warning: The issue with the next stretch is there are several hills between Obermuhl and Cresky Krumlov. Expect about 25 miles of moderate hills.
  - The ride from the lake at Horni Lana is quite enjoyable to Cresky Krumlov. 46 miles.
    - Option: If starting in Cresky Krumlov, consider doing the ride south to Horni Lana as a day trip along the Vltava river, reaching the Lipno Lake, leaving your bags in your hotel in Cresky Krumlov, and taking a train back at the end of the day.
o Cresky Krumlov is a beautiful small historic city.
  - Strong Recommendation.
    - This is one of my favorite small towns in Europe, listed on UNESCO world cultural heritage towns.
    - We had a wonderful stay at the Hotel Konvice, www.en.stadthotel-krummau.de, meeting the Walbrunn family that runs the hotel and the excellent restaurant.
  - Spend two nights in the city. It is especially charming late in the day after the tour buses leave!
o From Cresky Krumlov, head north. Ride to Creske Budejovice, 23 miles.
  - Note: This is the site of the original Budweiser beer, and a good overnight.
  - Options:
    - Take train to Prague from here, depending on your time available.

Cesky Krumlov Moldau River

- Continue Ride North. **Warning**: The route north does involve some hills, not huge climbing, but considerable up and down riding.
  o If riding north, head to Pisek, 32 miles, interesting stop if you would like time in smaller town.
  o Pisek to Prague is 82 miles.
    - This distance can be addressed by finding a stop at one of the many small towns along the route, using trains, or riding a big day.
    - Potential overnight stops in quite small towns include Kamyknad Vtavou or Von Celina.
  o **Extension Options:**
    - Vienna Option:
      - There is also a route, known at the Greenway, that will connect Cesky Krumlov to Vienna if you are looking for more riding! About 250 Miles.

Hamburg North Sea Extension

Interesting different scenery and culture in the north, and a good addition if in Hamburg, but even better if combine with Wesel River:

Interesting: ***

Navigation: **

Challenging: **

Ride Highlights

Ride along the North Sea.

See the North German beach areas.

Bremen

Brenhaven

Cuxhaven

Stade

Hamburg North Sea Extension

Miles and Days

96 to 176 Miles

Esterbauer Book(s) Needed

Elbe River Trail (2) English

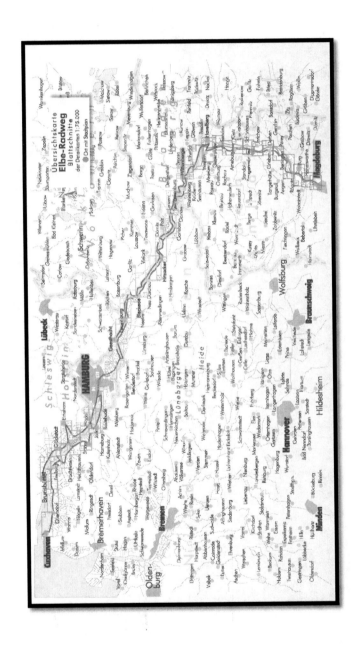

Hamburg North Sea Extension

Ride Features

o   This is a great 2 to 4 day extension that can be added on to a start in Hamburg.
o   Extend the trip by taking train from Hamburg to Bremen, Bremerhaven, or Cuxhaven to start your ride, depending on how long you have for this extra riding.
  - Bremen to Bremerhaven. 47 Miles. Part or all of this route can be by boat if you feel like a change of pace.
    - Recommendation:
      o   Visit the Climate Museum in Bremerhaven, quite unusual. The Maritime Museum is also interesting.
      o   If you have the budget, consider the Atlantis hotel, with its great views.
  - Bremerhaven to the Beaches. There are several towns to stop along this route, from Sahlenburg to Cuxhaven. Bremerhaven to Cuxhaven, 34 Miles.
  - Cuxhaven to Stade. 60 Miles, or consider taking a train from Cuxhaven to Otterndorf, and start your ride there, reducing the total ride by 15 miles.
  - Stade to Hamburg. 36 Miles. Explore Hamburg, a very interesting city.

Berlin Extension

If on Elbe and want to see Berlin this is the answer, but not as well-marked trail so a bit more challenging yet manageable. Berlin is 5 stars on interest, and there are some interesting aspects of the ride otherwise, from the empty forests to Potsdam:

Interesting: ****

Navigation: ****

Challenging: **

Ride Highlights

Extension from the Elbe River routes.

This route takes you from Wittenberg to Berlin.

Travel through quiet areas that used to serve as a buffer between East and West, before German reunification.

Wittenberg

Potsdam

Berlin

Berlin Extension

Miles and Days

2 Days, 80 Miles

Esterbauer Book(s) Needed

Europe-Radweg (R1)
- Note: The Europe Radweg can take you from Arnhem to Berlin.

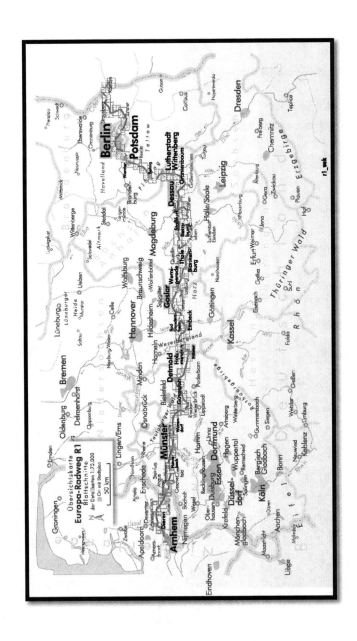

Forest Trail between Elbe and Potsdam Approach

Cycling Along Europe's Rivers

Caputh near Potsdam

New Palace in Potsdam

Berlin Extension

Entering Berlin

Checkpoint Charlie

Berlin, Old and New

Berlin Extension

Ride Features

- This route takes you off the Elbe River toward Berlin.
- Head out of Wittenberg on largely unpaved path. There are also roads, but the bike route is unpaved.
- Wittenberg to Potsdam. 49 Miles.
  - Wittenberg to Belzig. 25 Miles, a potential stop. Bring snacks and water for this ride, not many stops. Very quiet route.
  - Belzig to Potsdam. 24 Miles.
- Recommendation:
  - Caputh is an attractive small town just before Potsdam and its multiple lakes, with several fine hotels.
  - We enjoyed our stay at the Mullerhof Hotel, a hotel since 1889, although updated considerably, with its excellent restaurant. www.hotel-muellerhof.de. Reserve ahead if you know your ETA.
- Potsdam to Berlin. 30 Miles. Ride through Potsdam, and explore its historic buildings and museums, before heading to Berlin. You can ride directly into Berlin from Potsdam, which feels exciting as you enter this large city.
- **Options:**
  - Fly home from Berlin. In this case, you should have a hotel reservation near the airport. At the beginning of the trip you should have mailed your bike box to that hotel and advised them to hold the box until your arrival.
  - Fly home from Hamburg. Take train back to Hamburg, with trains that will accept bikes taking about two hours. This is a good option since easy to fly roundtrip from Hamburg and also leave your bike box at a hotel near the Hamburg airport. If you started your ride from Prague, you would want to have mailed your bike box to your hotel from the Prague airport.
  - Take train to Prague, although that can exceed 12 hours!

Cycling Along Europe's Rivers

Northern Europe

Weser River and Elbe Hamburg Loop

A terrific route, one of our favorite in the north combining part of the Elbe, providing a variety of storybook history and larger industrial cities, smaller rivers, and great ports:

Interesting: *****

Navigation: **

Challenging: **

Ride Highlights

This is an interesting and varied route around northern Germany through small towns and some of the major port cities in Europe.

Visit the region that is called the Fairy Tale Road, home of Sleeping Beauty, the Pied Piper, Cinderella, Rapunzel, Hansel and Gretel, Little Ride Riding Hood, and Snow White -- Brothers Grimm and others.

Travel along a very small river that gradually is transformed into a very large river at the mouth of the North Sea.

Mostly German tourists in this region, not as many "international" tourists.

Good train and boats infrastructure generally.

Hann. Munden, Bremen, Bremerhaven. Hoxter, Hamelin, Stade, Hamburg.

The North Sea, Cuxhaven and Beaches.

Given the climate, try and do this ride in early August-July, hope to avoid the rain, but be prepared for it!

Cycling Along Europe's Rivers

Miles and Days

320 Miles from Hann. Munden to Cuxhaven.
96 Miles from Cuxhaven to Hamburg.
9-Plus Days

Esterbauer Book(s) Needed

Weser-Radweg
Elbe River Trail (2) in English

Weser River and Elbe Hamburg Loop

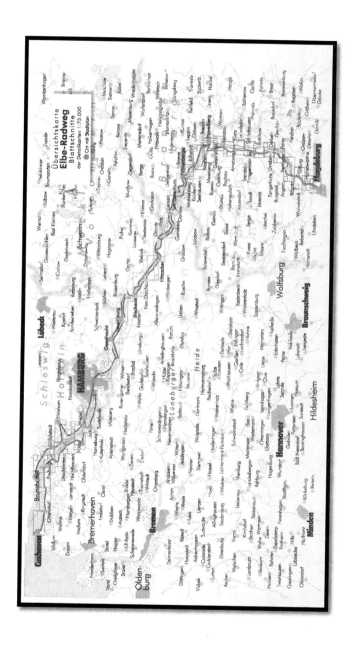

Cycling Along Europe's Rivers

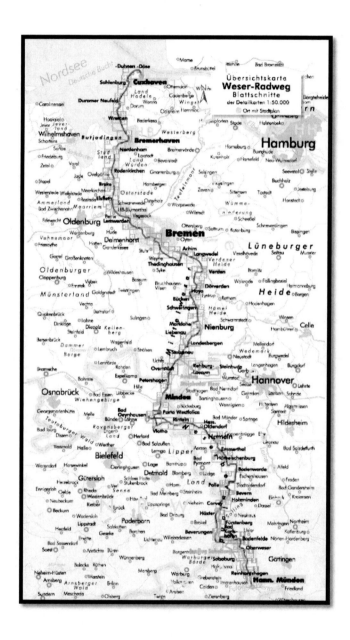

Weser River and Elbe Hamburg Loop

Ride from Gottingen to Hann. Munden

Hann. Munden

View from Hotel Peter in Reinhardshagan

Along the Weser

Weser River and Elbe Hamburg Loop

Hoxter

Monastery in Corvey

Along the Weser

Weser Trail

Weser River and Elbe Hamburg Loop

Baron Munchhausen in Bodenwerder

Pied Piper in Hameln

Cycling Along Europe's Rivers

Sharing the Road

Weser Widening Toward Its Mouth

Weser River and Elbe Hamburg Loop

Hotel Atlantic in Bremerhavan

Bremerhavan Maritime Museum

Cycling Along Europe's Rivers

Docks North of Bremerhavan

Low Tide on North Sea and Unusual Carriage Trips

Weser River and Elbe Hamburg Loop

Cuxhavan and Mouth of the Elbe

Stade

Entering Hamburg from the North

Lake in Hamburg

Weser River and Elbe Hamburg Loop

New Hamburg Development

Ride Features

- Fly roundtrip into Hamburg. Upon arrival, leave bike boxes at hotel that you have reserved ahead of time. One hotel is the Mercure near Hamburg Airport.
- Ride to center of Hamburg, or take the train from the airport.
- There are several ways to start this ride — train to Gottingen and ride, train all the way to Hann. Munden, or even ride from Hamburg.
    - Options:
        - Take train from Hamburg to Gottingen.
            - If you had enough for the day, stay in Gottingen, since this is a long day already.
        - Take train to Hann. Munden changing trains in Gottingen.
        - Ride from Hamburg to Gottingen
            - 212 Miles

- Reasonably flat, but not entirely.
    - Bikeline: Leine-Heide-Radweg.
  o Recommendation:
    - Hann. Mundenis a beautiful medieval small town, and a great stop for the night.
- If starting in Gottingen, the ride to Hann. Munden is about 19 miles of riding through quite countryside, **but many hills**(1200 vertical total climb)! Having a map of the area, or a GPS, is useful, since this section is not covered by the Bikeline guide. The roads are well-marked, so if you have several smaller towns as targets, it is not a difficult ride.
- Once in Hann. Munden, and heading north, the first part of this ride is the German Fairytale Trail.
- If you stayed in Gottingen and are looking for an easy first day, consider Reinhardshagan (9 miles past Hann. Munden), about 28 miles from Gottingen, through Hann. Munden (lunch in Hann. Munden.)
  o Recommendation:
    - Hotel Peter, with nice, well-priced rooms overlooking the river, a quiet stop, not an interesting town.www.hotel-peter.net.
    - Special Option: If you have the time, don't mind a climb from the river to the surrounding hilly forest, and have the budget, consider the 650 year old Castle Hotel Sababurg, said to be the inspiration for Sleeping Beauty. The route is provided in the Bikeline book maps 24-25. The detour route through the hills rejoins the river at Bad Karlshafen. Note: Staying at the Castle Hotel is also an option if starting from Hann. Munden, just a short first day of riding, but then there is the climb to consider!
- If starting from Hann. Munden, then ride to Hoxter. 47 Miles.
  o Recommendation: Ringhotel Niedersachsen, more expensive than our typical hotels, but a good stay. www.hoexter.ringhotels.de.
  o Boat Option:

Weser River and Elbe Hamburg Loop

- Take a boat part of the way, with the Weserfahrten running from Bad Karlshafen to Oedeisheim.www.weserschiff-linie2000.de.
- Another company runs boats for various routes from Bad Karlshafen all the way to Bremen. Look at schedules and consider segments. www.flotte-wesser.de.
- Hoxter to Hameln. 48 Miles. After visiting the Monastery in Corvey, ride to Polle for a break. Spend time at Hameln, the site of the Pied Piper Story.
  - o Recommendation:
    - Stop at the historic Monastery in Corvey on the way out of Hoxter.
- Hameln to Minden or Bad Oeynhausen. 38-43 Miles.
  - o Route Options:
    - Consider taking a train from Minden to Hannover, and then riding back to the river past Steinhude and its attractive lake, and rejoining the alternative route in the Bikeline Guide near Schusselburg.
    - Also consider riding from Minden to Hannover, and then back to the trail through Steinhude if time permits.
  - o Recommendation:
    - If looking for lunch or snack in Minden, try the Cafe Lenz.www.dompraline.de.
- Minden to Nienburg.38 Miles.
  - o Recommendation:
    - Hotel Weserschlosschen, right on the river. Good value and setting. www.weserschloesschen.de/en/
- Nienburg to Verden. 35 Miles. It is possible to ride Minden to Verden if you are in a hurry and can handle the mileage (73 Miles). In Verden, consider the Thoeles hotel, simple, new, clean rooms.www.thoeles.de.

Cycling Along Europe's Rivers

- Verden to Bremen. 29 Miles. Leave time to explore Bremen, so getting in for lunch is a good option.
  - Recommendation:
    - The Ratswinkeller Restaurant has been serving food for over 600 years — great atmosphere! A UNESCO World Heritage Site. Said to be German's oldest town hall restaurant. Make reservations for a private booth for dinner.
    - Consider the Ibis Bremen Centrum. Hotels can be costly in Bremen, and this hotel provides clean, simple, modern rooms in good location.
- Bremen to Bremerhaven. 47 Miles.
  - Option:
    - Consider taking a boat all or part of this distance for a change, or if one rider wants to have an easier day. Boat line: www.hal-oever.de.
  - Recommendation:
    - Visit the Climate Museum in Bremerhaven, quite unusual. The Maritime Museum is also interesting.www.klimahaus-bremerhaven.de.
    - If you have the budget, consider the Atlantis hotel, with its great views.www.atlantic-hotels.de.
    - Consider a sailing trip on the "Running on Waves" for a night or more, if time. www.sailingaway24.de.
- Bremerhaven to the Beaches. There are several towns to stop at along this route, from Sahlenburg to Cuxhaven. 34 Miles from Bremerhaven to Cuxhaven.
- Cuxhaven to Stade. 60 Miles, or consider taking a train from Cuxhaven to Otterndorf, and riding the rest, reducing the total ride by 15 miles.
- Stade to Hamburg. 36 Miles. Explore Hamburg, a very interesting city. Spend two nights if you can, including the last night near the airport. It is possible to ride from the center of Hamburg to the airport, riding past the central lake, about 10 Miles.
  - Recommendation:

Weser River and Elbe Hamburg Loop

- Take a ride around Hamburg, especially the central lake and the surrounding historic areas. A ride to the waterfront and the new dock area is also interesting.
- Visit the Beatles early-years sites.
- Consider timing your trip to be in Hamburg during the Classics bike race, usually in mid-August. Reserve hotel ahead if you come during this event.
- Motel One chain has a few hotels in Hamburg, and tend to be good values. Simple, clean, modern all you need. Call ahead a week or more to see if there is anything happening in Hamburg — big meetings or events can cause hotel supply to disappear.
- **Extension Options:**
    - There are several options for this ride.
    - Note: I have not completed either of these rides mentioned below, but they looked interesting and are on my short list!
        - **Fulda Bike Route:**
            - Fulda-Radweg Esterbauer Book.
            - 110 Miles.
            - Ride the river south of Hann. Munden.
            - See more of the Fairy-Tale Road.
            - Possible to fly into Frankfurt if you use this extension. Fly home from Frankfurt, or mail bike box to hotel near Hamburg airport.
                - Note: Can take frequent train from Frankfurt to Fulda, about one hour and twenty minutes, and fly home from Hamburg, or take train from Hamburg to Frankfurt.

Cycling Along Europe's Rivers

- Start: Take train to Gersfeld and head north along the Fulda River, with the route from Gersfeld downhill to Fulda.

Weser River and Elbe Hamburg Loop

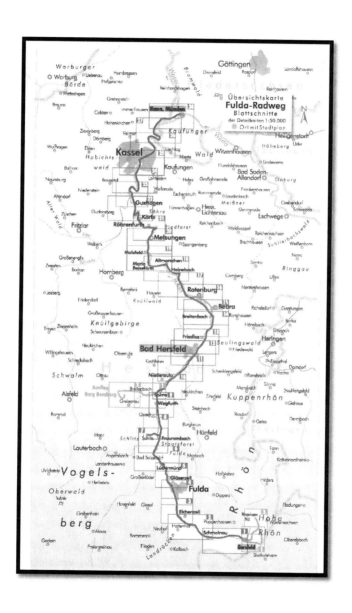

o **Other Options:**

- Extending the ride by flying into Hamburg and either:
  - Riding south on the Elbe to Magdelburg, then riding to Hann. Munden or taking a train across.
  - Riding on the trail from Hamburg to Hannover, then riding to Hann. Munden or taking train to Hann. Munden or Gottingen and starting the ride north on the Weser.
    - o Use Bikeline: Leine-Heide-Radweg
    - o 250 Miles from Hamburg past Hanover to Leinhfeld.
      - Hamburg to Hanover, 133 Miles
      - Hamburg to Gottingen, 212 Miles.

Amsterdam to Hamburg

I have only done the beginning and second half of this ride, but looks like a good outing, especially with the wind at your back riding from Amsterdam to Hamburg:

Interesting: ****

Navigation: ***

Challenging: **

Ride Highlights

The North Sea

Holland and Germany Visited

Amsterdam

Bremen

Bremerhaven

Stade

Hamburg

Miles and Days

Amsterdam to Nieweschans. 200 Miles.

Nieuweschans to Hamburg. 325 Miles.

Cycling Along Europe's Rivers

Esterbauer Book(s) Needed

Nordseekusten-Radweg(1)
Nordseekusten-Radweg (2)

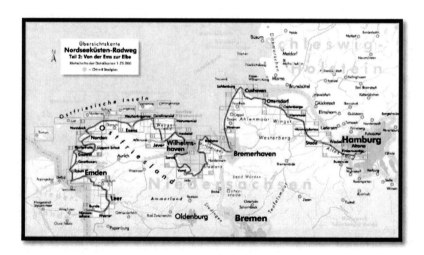

Amsterdam to Hamburg

Ride Features

- Fly into Amsterdam, head East.
- Ride from Amsterdam to Bremen.
  - Note: I have not completed this segment from Amsterdam to Bremen, so will not go into detail here, but it looked interesting and thought it would be worth mentioning.
  - Make sure you ride with the wind behind you since it can be intense in this area.
  - Also, don't ride too late in the summer since it gets cooler, and more rain.
- Bremen to Bremerhaven. 47 Miles. Part or all of this route can be by boat if you feel like a change of pace.
  - Recommendation
    - Visit the Climate Museum in Bremerhaven, quite unusual.
    - The Maritime Museum is also interesting.
    - If you have the budget, consider the Atlantis hotel, with its great views.
- Bremerhaven to the Beach. There are several towns to stop along this route, from Sahlenburg to Cuxhaven. Miles from Bremerhaven to Cuxhaven 34 Miles.
- Cuxhaven to Stade. 60 Miles, or consider taking a train from Cuxhaven to Otterndorf, and then riding the rest, reducing the ride by 15 miles.
- Stade to Hamburg. 36 Miles. Explore Hamburg, a very interesting city. It is possible to ride from the center of Hamburg to the airport, riding past the central lake, about 10 Miles.
  - Recommendation:
    - Take a ride around Hamburg, especially the central lake and the surrounding historic areas. A ride to the waterfront and the new dock area is also interesting.
    - Spend at least two nights in Hamburg.

Italy

Po River: Milan to Venice

One of the few flat trail rides in Italy, so if you want to ride in Italy with an easy, flat, trip, this is a good choice. A bit off the beaten path, cities you might not go to otherwise, not many international tourists until Venice. River is easy to follow, but probably the least attractive river in the book given the pollution we saw in the river (2005):

Interesting: ****

Navigation: ***

Challenging: *

Ride Highlights

Opportunity to ride in Italy without hills and mostly on a trail, or quiet roads. (Most riding in Italy tends to involve hills!)

The Po River is certainly not the most attractive river in Europe.

Fair infrastructure, rail not available everywhere and no boats during my ride.

Interesting Italian towns that are not often visited by foreign tourists (except for Venice).

Milan, Piacenza, Cremona, Parma, Mantua, Lido.

Venice: Riding there along the Lido and taking a boat into Venice to finish the trip is an exciting experience!

Po River: Milan to Venice

Miles and Days

360 Miles
9 Days Plus

Esterbauer Book(s) Needed

Po-Radweg

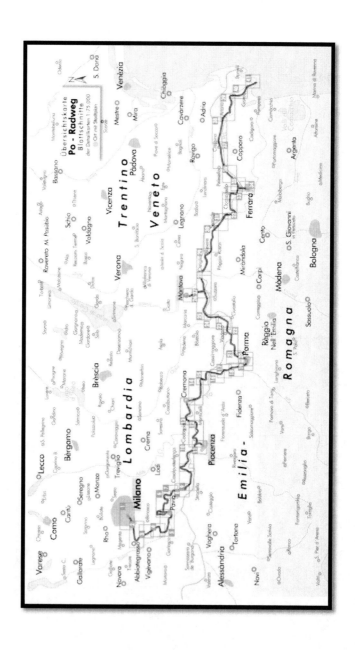

Po River: Milan to Venice

Naviglio di Bereguardo

German WW2 Pontoon Bridge

Rebuilt Bridge in Pavia

Monastery at Certosa di Pavia

Po River: Milan to Venice

On the Trail

Cremona and Stradivarius

Piacenza

Mantua

Po River: Milan to Venice

Po River

Castle at Ferrara

Cycling Along Europe's Rivers

Beautiful Chioggia

Approach to Venice from Lido

Po River: Milan to Venice

Venice

Cycling Along Europe's Rivers

Ride Features

- Fly into Milan.
- This is designed as a one-way tour, although you can take a train back from Venice to Milan and do a roundtrip flight from Milan.
- Reserve hotel in Venice before trip, and ship bike box from Milan to Venice hotel.
- Milan to Pavia. 40 Miles. Night in Pavia.
- Pavia to Piacenza. 60 Miles. Night in Piacenza.
- Piacenza to Cremona, 36 Miles.
  - Recommendation: Visit the home of Stradivari and the music museum.
- Cremona to Parma, 44 Miles. Parma is home to one of the oldest universities in the world, founded in 1117. Night in Parma.
- Parma to Mantua, 56 Miles. Mantua (Mantova) is one of the nicest cities on the ride, with multiple lakes, interesting architecture, and museums. Night in Mantua.
- Mantua to Ostiglia, 33 Miles Night in Ostiglia.
- Ostiglia to Ferrara, 43 Miles. Night in Ferra.
  - Option: Long ride from Mantova to Ferrara, 77 Miles.
- Ferrara to Ariano, 34 Miles.
  - Options:
  - This is where I exit the Bikeline route, although you can continue to the Po Delta, about another 20 miles, then double back to stay in Berra or another location.
  - Can stay in Berra, a few miles short of Ariano.
  - Can decide not to stop, and continue to ride, crossing the river at Ariano, and heading north to Adria on small country roads, crossing the river again at Mazzomo. Total Ariano to Adria approximately 10 miles. Stay in Adria.
  - Ride from Adria to Chioggia, 20 Miles, on small country roads, using GPS and compass (I did it with only a compass, not that difficult, generally north direction passed Cavarzere).Quiet roads.
    - Option: Take a short train ride between the cities.

Po River: Milan to Venice

- o Consider spending night in the surprising delightful town of Chioggia — surprising, since I had never heard of this city before the trip!
- Chioggia to Venice, 17 Miles.
  - o Recommendation: Great ride along the outer barrier islands, ending in the Lido, where a boat can take you to Venice, or spend a night on the Lido at one of the beach hotels.
- Spend time in Venice, at least 2 nights, but 2-3 full days can be filled easily in Venice.
- Take boat from your island in Venice to the airport with your bike!
  - o Don't pack your bike in box before getting to airport, too difficult with the boats to take a packed box.

- **Etsch River (Adige River) Extension Option:**
  - o The Po River ride comes close to Verona near Mantova, providing a connection to the Etsch-Radweg, described below.
  - o This extension provides an opportunity to start in the Alps, ride down to Verona. Ride or train to Mantova, continue on the Po, then finish in Venice.

Etsch River Bike Trail: Landeck Switzerland to Verona

Start in the mountains and end in Venice, plenty of interest, but not a traditional river route like most in the book:

Interesting: ***

Navigation: **

Challenging: ***

Ride Highlights

Etsch River (also known as the Adige River)

Landeck

Meran

Bozen

Trento

Verona

Connection to the Po River Route and to Venice.

Miles and Days

210 Miles

Esterbauer Book(s) Needed

Etsch-Radweg

Etsch River Bike Trail

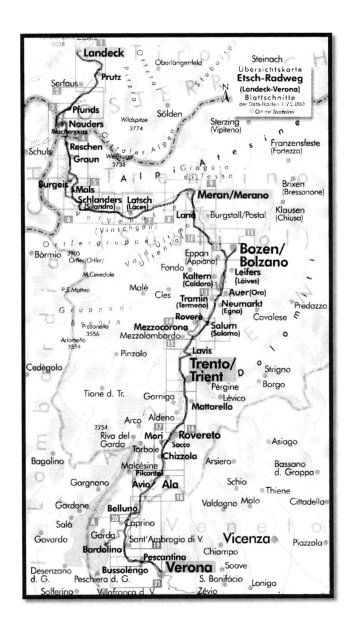

Ride Features

- Note: I have not completed this ride, so will not go into detail. But it looks interesting, and if you are seeking other rides in Italy, especially rides that connect to other rides in this book, consider this route.
- Consider starting near Nauders and ride generally downhill to Verona.
- See potential connection to Po River described in Po River Section.

France

Loire River: Orleans to St Nazaire

One of my favorite routes, great sites and food, but more challenging than others in the book — worth it if you are ready (don't want to scare you, this is a terrific route, and very doable, but more complicated than the Rhine or Elbe, for example):

Interesting: *****

Navigation: ****

Challenging: ****

Ride Highlights

One of my favorite rides, although not the easiest. It is a ride to do, but not the first ride you do in Europe.

More complicated navigation and many times off the river and on quiet roads.

With GPS and the new trail markers installed since I did this ride in 2004, should make this ride easier.

Great history and scenery

Castles and Chateaus, too numerous to list.

Amazing Meals and Snacks, of course.

Interesting historic hotels.

Paris, Orleans, Blois, Tours, Saumur, Angers, Nantes, Amboise

St. Nazaire, and the German Submarine Pens.

La Baule and the Atlantic Beach.

Cycling Along Europe's Rivers

Miles and Days

300 Miles Plus
10 Days Plus

Esterbauer Book(s) Needed

Loire-Radweg

Loire River: Orleans to St Nazaire

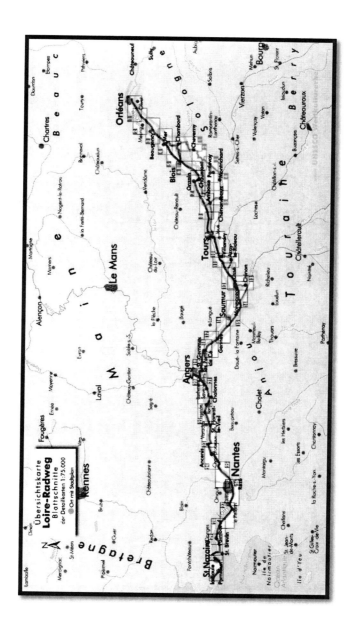

St. Dye Sur Loire, the Small Loire River

Along the Loire Trail

Loire River: Orleans to St Nazaire

View of the Loire

Chateau de Chinon

Chateau de Chambord

Chateau de Chenonceau

Loire River: Orleans to St Nazaire

Along the Loire

Chateau de Villandry

Cycling Along Europe's Rivers

Enjoying an Old Grape Press

Parking in Medieval Stables, Hotel Chateau de Prey, Amboise

Loire River: Orleans to St Nazaire

900 Year Old House, Now B&B

Crossing the Loire

Cycling Along Europe's Rivers

Loire River

Angers Castle

Loire River: Orleans to St Nazaire

Near the End of the Loire

Loire Delta

Loire Delta

Tough Climb, St-Nazaire Bridge

Loire River: Orleans to St Nazaire

St. Nazaire and German WW2 Submarine Pens

La Baule beach on the Atlantic Ocean

Arc de Triomphe and a Ride Through Paris

Loire River: Orleans to St Nazaire

Ride Features

- This is a great ride, but is a bit more complicated and demanding than most, because it involves leaving the river and undertaking some hills if you want to see some of the central sites of the route, especially certain chateaus and castles.
- Start this ride by flying into Paris. Reserve a hotel near the airport, and leave your bike box there upon arrival.
- Get to Orleans to start the ride.
  - One way is to take the train to central Paris, and take a train to Orleans. The trains run regularly, but you need to be careful to find trains that can take bikes. Check with the airport information desk upon arrival.
  - Alternatively, rent a small van and driver to take you and your group directly to Orleans. I did that last trip, more expensive, but if you have a few people, it is worth the reduction in hassle.
- Stay the night in Orleans, and explore. It is also possible to take a day ride toward Chateauneuf (the opposite direction of our route) for a short warm-up ride.
- **Key Route Option**: It is necessary that you make a determination whether to ride along the river as much as possible, which is an easier route generally, or take side trips away from the river to see some of the most famous chateaus.
  - Recommendation: Since these chateaus are so fantastic, I would recommend leaving the river for these side routes, and that is what is outlined below.
- Orleans to St Dye sur Loire. 32 Miles. This is a pleasant small town for an overnight.
  - Option: Ride an additional 3 miles to Chambord and spend the night. You might like to reserve a hotel ahead for this city, can be more expensive and crowded.
- St Dye sur Loire to Amboise. 52 Miles.
  - Take the alternative route toward Chambord, visit the Chateau. Here I recommend taking the alternative route to Chenonceaux.

- ○ Next to Chateau de Villesavin, about 5.5 miles.
- ○ Next to Chateau de Cheverny, about 8 miles.
- ○ Next to Fougeressur Bievre, about 13.5 miles.
- ○ Next to Amboise and through various sites, about 24.5 miles.
- ○ Options: A ride of 52 Miles in itself is not bad, and this is what we did our last trip. But it was an exhausting day, not just the miles and the hills, but all the amazing sites that we needed to rush through.
  - Recommendation: If you have time, find a stop along this route for a night, and take your time. Possibly reserve ahead near one of the great sites.
- Amboise. This is one of my favorite towns on the route. Great sites, including the castle and the Clos-Luce with its fascinating Leonardo da Vinci exhibits.
  - ○ Recommendation:
    - If you have time, consider two nights in Amboise. If not, consider a stop along the route to Amboise, as recommended above, and get to Amboise early in the day so you have as much time as possible to look around.
    - The Chateau de Prey Hotel is one of my favorite hotels of all the rides, but also one of the more expensive places I have stayed. Usually over $250 per night (not in itself outrageous in many contexts, but more than I budget for these trips).If you are going to spend one night in this range, consider this stop. When else do you get a chance to stay in a hotel from 1224 that has suits of armor from the original owners in the hallway! www.praycastel.online.fr.
- Option: If you have time, consider a ride back to Blois, which amounts to backtracking toward Orleans, since this is an interesting city missed by taking the inland chateau route. This also provides a chance to visit the Chateau de Chaumont. It is about 28 miles from Amboise to Blois, providing an opportunity for an easy day and time to visit the sites along the way and Blois.

The next morning take a train back to Amboise and continue the trip — or ride back if time.

- Amboise to Tours. 19 Miles. Tours is a good lunch stop. Can also stay overnight, but depends on timing. If you do the trip back to Blois, as discussed above, and then ride from Blois to Tours the next day, that would be 47 Miles and a good ride.
- Tours to Langeais. 21 Miles. If riding from Amboise, Langeais makes a good overnight, with 40 mile total day. Stops along the route include the Chateau de Villandry.
  - Option: If you want to do more riding this day, can ride to Azay le Rideau. Or do this section on the way out of Langeais the next morning. About 6 miles each way from the river.
    - Recommendation: The Azay le Rideau Chateau is worth the extra riding.
- Langeais to Saumur.39 Miles. Overnight in Saumur.
  - Ride to Azay if have not done so yet, then to Chinon. Langeais to Chinon, 16.5 miles.
  - Then 14 miles to Montsoreau.
  - There is an option here to visit the Abby Royal.
  - Montsoreau to Saumur. 8 miles.
  - Option:
    - Ride an additional 13 miles to Gennes. Stay in the Domaine de Joreau, a pleasant country bed and breakfast, for a different experience away from the crowds.
- Saumur to Gennes. 13 Miles.
- Gennes to Angers. 27 Miles. Overnight in Angers if riding from Saumur.
- Angers to Montjeansur Loire. 25 Miles. 52 Miles from Saumur makes this a good stop, but nothing remarkable. It was our overnight last trip.
    - Option: Consider train and skipping this section if time is short.
- Montjean to Loire Ancenis, 18 Miles. Visit St Florent le Vieil on the way.

Cycling Along Europe's Rivers

- Ancenies to Nantes. 25 Miles. Overnight in Nantes. Total Montjean to Nantes, 43 Miles. Explore Nantes.
- Nantes to Paimboeuf. 28 Miles. The ride gets very flat as the Loire widens approaching the sea.
- Paimboeuf to St.Nazaire. 15. Miles.
  - Options. Much of this ride is quite easy and quiet, but there is probably the toughest section in this book ahead — the Pont de St. Nazaire. A giant bridge, that was not at all bike friendly. Very steep, very little shoulder. Slow going up as cars hurl by, and the ride down took us all over 30 mph the entire stretch. It was one of those amazing riding experiences, but one I would probably avoid next time. **Note**: There are reports that the bridge has recently been made more bike-friendly, so check for current conditions. Also consider finding another way, such as:
    - A van to take you across (not easy to arrange).
    - Stop in Coeron, and take a short train ride to St Nazaire.
      - Recommendation: If you are with kids or other riders that are not very strong and fearless, take this train!
- Stay overnight in St.Nazaire. St. Nazaire is an interesting city given the historic WW2 German submarine pens and museum that can be explored. The allies tried repeatedly to bomb this place off the map and conducted an incredible raid to destroy the German dry-docks. Although largely put out of commission, the German's did not surrender the city until after the fall of Berlin!
  - Option: If time, consider a ride to La Baule Escoublac, about 11 miles, and stay a night in this seaside resort and enjoying the beach before returning to Paris.
- Take a train from St.Nazaire to Paris. The problem here is that last time we did this trip the high-speed trains would not accept bikes. If this is the case, the trip can take quite a long time. Check with French rail before the trip to find current options.
- Paris. Consider a day of riding around Paris. Riding from the Arch de Triumph down the Camps-Elysees is quite an experience!

Grand Circle Tour

Grand Circle Tour: Central and Western Europe Connecting the Rhine, Elbe, and Danube Rivers

I wish I had time to do this entire route — but that is why I have spent nearly 20 years taking a week or two in Europe doing segments!

Interesting: *****

Navigation: ****

Challenging: ***

Ride Highlights

See the best of all the routes offered in this book, visiting Germany, the Netherlands, Austria, Hungary, the Czech Republic, Switzerland, and France.

This ride connects the three core rivers outlined in this book: the Rhine, the Elbe, and the Danube.

If you are looking for a 3-month plus ride in Europe — such as a full summer trip — consider this route.

Too many highlights to list again here, but use the various rides in this book for more details.

Cycling Along Europe's Rivers

Miles and Days

This is a full summer and more of riding.

Esterbauer Book(s) Needed

Rhine-Radweg (Volumes 1-3)
Main-Radweg
Mosel River Trail (English)
Neckar-Radweg
Elbe-Radweg (1-2)
Danube-Radweg (1-3)
Nordseekusten- Radweg (1-2)
Moldau Radweg
Weser Radweg

Grand Circle Tour

Ride Features

- Where you start could depend on what time of year you begin your trip.
- I would recommend Northern Europe mid-July through mid-August.
- Keep the wind direction in mind when planning, especially in Northern Europe.
- If going longer than the summer, would recommend riding into the Fall rather than starting too early in the Spring. This will give you a better chance of minimizing rain.
- Even though this is a long trip, I would still travel light, with only rear panniers, if possible, and build in laundry days. Less is more in cycling to me, although many people decide to ride fully loaded. Don't be afraid to ship things home, throw things out and buy new things when needed, and don't bulk up the bike! Also consider sending some supplies to hotels in later parts of the trip. For example, maybe send supplies to Budapest as a way to get a change of clothes, and deal with different climates. Mail what you are not using home.
- Consider additional routes that can be added on, such as the Loire River and the Po River, to have more variety and visit additional countries — and enjoy more types of food!
- There are also other interesting routes in the Bikeline series if you have more time for additional rides, especially in Eastern Europe.
- The general Grand Route might look something like this:
    - Fly into Amsterdam.
    - Head east along the North Sea Route toward Bremen.
    - At Bremen, consider a train south to Hann. Munden and ride back up the Weser River.
    - Continue from Bremen to Cuxhaven, then down the Elbe, past Hamburg.
    - Consider a side trip to Berlin. There are also other rides from Berlin, not covered in this book, including to Copenhagen (but a bit hilly).
    - Continue down the Elbe to Prague.

Cycling Along Europe's Rivers

- Take the Moldau trail to Cresky Kumlov.
- From here you could go all the way south to the Danube near Passau in Austria, or take the Greenway trail toward Vienna, and join the Danube at Vienna.
- On the Danube consider riding to at least Budapest, although that would take you a bit out of the loop— but worth it. If go to Budapest, could also add Lake Balaton. It is also possible to continue to the Black Sea on the Danube.
- The circle continues back at Vienna and heads west along the Danube.
- At the headwaters of the Danube, traverse the hills to get to Lake Bodensee and spend time enjoying and touring the Lake.
- Consider a side trip at this point to Italy, including riding the Etsch to the Po, and then to Venice. It is also possible to add a side trip on the Romantische Strassa (Romantic Road), which stretches from Fussen to Wurzburg. I would ride from Fussen north, so heading more downhill. Not a river, so not covered in this book.
- Then head up the Rhine, north. Many stops along this 760 mile trail.
- There are also several side rides outlined in the book, such as the Mosel, the Neckar, and the Main.
- If you ride the Mosel, at the end of that ride in the east, could train to the beginning of the Loire River route for another excursion.
- Back on the Rhine head north and finish in Amsterdam.
- Finish this, and make everyone jealous!

Day Ride Options

Finally, here is a brief section covering several locations that serve as especially attractive day ride hubs.

Advantages:

- These cities provide the opportunity to stay in one hotel for multiple nights, and take day rides without panniers.
- These locations are also interesting venues for non-riders to spend time while riders are on the tour.
- Easier logistics than many rides.
- Some cities can be combined to make an entire trip (Koblenz and Trier can make a great trip).
- Note: Double check train/boat connections on all rides.

Koblenz:

Koblenz on the Rhine can be reached easily from Frankfurt Airport and provides the opportunity for the following day rides:

- North on the Rhine, 40 miles to Bonn, and train or boat back.
- South on the Rhine, 40 miles to Rudesheim, and train or boat back.
- On Mosel, to Cochem and/or Eltz Castle, 30-45 miles.
- On Lahn River starting near Lahnstein, to Limburg 40 miles, check connections.

Cycling Along Europe's Rivers

Trier:

Trier, on the Mosel, can be combined with Koblenz as two cities that each provide multiple days of riding, connected by train ride that is less than 2 hours between the cities:

- Luxembourg City (48 miles), and other shorter routes available.
- Down the Saar River to Saarburg, Mettlach and the beautiful Saarchleife. (Bikeline "Velo Route SaarLor Lux" Book useful.)(30 miles).
- South on the Mosel to Perl or Thionville (55 miles).
- North on the Mosel to Bernkastel-Kues (37 miles) or Traban-Trabach (50 miles).

Lake Bodensee:

Lake Bodensee provides opportunity for multiple rides staying in 2-3 different cities, including Meersburg, Konstanz, and Chur. See the section in the book on Lake Bodensee.

Passau:

Passau can be combined with Lake Bodensee, and provides several day rides, and is easy to reach from Munich:

- West on the Danube to Straubing and train back, (55 miles).
- East on the Danube to Engelhartszell(32 Miles), take boat back to Passau.
- Down the Inn River to Burghausen. (54 Miles). Check on Train connections.
- Ilz River ride (Various Miles). Check train connections.

Conclusion

Touring Europe by bike is for everyone.

I hope you got some good ideas and inspiration for your next trip. There are many great ideas for trips in this book.

But also feel free to design your own routes — using some of the core route ideas outlined herein.

Enjoy, and be safe!

Appendix

Checklist

	Hotel Reservation night near final airport
	Bike Box (airline, purchased, Luftansa no box needed0
	BikeLine Books
	General Guidebook Sections
	Bike Tune Up, New Tires/Tubes (old tubes as spares), New Chain+Cassette
	GPS and/or Compass, Chargers if Necessary
	Bike Tools
	Helmet
	Travel Toilitries/Sun Tan Lotion
	Small Bike Pump
	Packing Tape
	Small First Aid Kit, Optional: Antibiotic, Benadryl for Bites
	Camera and Charger
	GSM Phone w/international roaming turned on with telecom carrier
	iTouch, iPad, or e-Reader Optional
	Riding Shirts (2)
	Riding Pants
	Riding Shoes
	Off Bike Shoes
	Underwear for each day
	Socks for each day
	Gortex-like lightweight rain coat, bright color
	Fleece sweat shirt
	Long sleeve shirt for off bike
	Long pants for off bike (zip off for shorts best)
	Hat
	Ziplock bags, 2.5 gallons
	Panniers that you have tested on your bike, fit, and which don't fall off
	Extra rack pack or handle pack
	Passport
	Sunglasses

ABOUT THE AUTHOR

Mike Lyon has been cycling for over 40 years, and has been touring in Europe through self-guided travel since 1994. He has also traveled extensively around-the-world, having visited over 90 countries for both work and pleasure.

When not cycling, Mike works with companies to assist them with developing and implementing international strategic plans and business (www.lyoncapitalservices.com). Mike was also a leader in the space tourism sector, where he worked extensively on organizing the first three flights of tourist who spent over $20 million to visit the International Space Station aboard Russian spacecraft (Dennis Tito and Mark Shuttleworth).

Mike also served in senior posts in the U.S. government, including as the Special Assistant to L. William Seidman at the Federal Deposit Insurance Corporation and Resolution Trust Corporation (U.S. Government Agencies) during America's Savings &Loan financial crisis, and as an Assistant Director for Resolutions at the RTC dealing with larger failed thrifts (over $500 million in assets).

Mike received his J.D. from the Harvard Law School, and his B.A. in History from Brandeis University. He also attended the London School of Economics.

Mike lives and cycles in the Washington, D.C. area, with his wife, Kusavadee, and son, Joshua – his great cycling companion.

Mike Along the Elbe River

Mike and Joshua Along Rhine River in Alps

CPSIA information can be obtained at www.ICGtesting.com
Printed in the USA
LVOW07s2124050314

376242LV00011B/153/P